The Christian Woman's GUIDE TO A BLESSED LIFE

The Christian Woman's
GUIDE TO A
BLESSED LIFE

Sharie L. Neal

Edited by SHARON Y. BROWN

Pleasant Word
A Division of WINEPRESS PUBLISHING

Packaged by Pleasant Word, PO Box 428, Enumclaw, WA 98022. The views expressed or implied in this work do not necessarily reflect those of Pleasant Word. The author(s) is ultimately responsible for the design, content and editorial accuracy of this work.

Unless otherwise noted, all Scriptures are taken from the Holy Bible, New International Version, Copyright © 1973, 1978, 1984 by the International Bible Society. Used by permission of Zondervan Publishing House. The "NIV" and "New International Version" trademarks are registered in the United States Patent and Trademark Office by International Bible Society.

Scripture references marked KJV are taken from the King James Version of the Bible.

Scripture references marked NASB are taken from the New American Standard Bible, © 1960, 1963, 1968, 1971, 1972, 1973, 1975, 1977 by The Lockman Foundation. Used by permission.

ISBN 1-4141-0329-8
Library of Congress Catalog Card Number: 2004098523

Dedication

*G*od has used the Holy Scriptures, Christian classics, and godly Christian men and women to teach, train, correct, encourage, and motivate me in the faith.

There are five women in particular whose lives have reflected God's will before me as a Christian woman, wife, and mother and to whom I would like to dedicate this work:

My grandmother, the late Angeline Glover Barnes, who with an eighth-grade education, demonstrated the essence of the Proverbs 31 woman. Through 60 years of marriage and eight children, she exercised an undying love and dedication to her family, strength of character, outstretched arms to the poor, wisdom, faith, and womanly propriety.

My mom, Dorothea E. Harris Gaulden who loved me sacrificially and by her example, instilled in me the importance of walking by faith, exercising diligence in my work ethic, and persevering with a good attitude.

My mother-in-law, Doris L. Neal, who lovingly nurtured and taught my husband Christian values as a boy. Who through 58 years of marriage and six children modeled before me the courage to dare to be different if that is what obeying Christ led me to be as a faithful wife and loving mom.

Patricia Richardson, my pastor's wife and director of our Women's Ministry, who mirrored a genuine love for the Lord, support for her husband and his call to ministry and an undying commitment to God's people.

Audree L. Ashe, who encouraged precision and modeled unwavering faith in the face of various life challenges.

Without these Christian women, who by believing God for me and taking me under their wings, my life would not be the same. I thank God for His plan for my life and that these faithful Christian women, through their obedience to Christ and godly example, were a part of that plan.

Table of Contents

Samples and Forms

Preface

$\mathcal{R}$egardless of their economic or working status, women (wives, mothers, single-parents, divorced, widowed, and adult children) of the twenty-first century are hurting. From women working on the corporate level to your stay-at-home mom, more and more women suffer from acid reflux and heart disease, depression and mental illness.

Two times more women than men suffer from depression and anxiety disorders.[1] Forty-four percent of women ages 18–44, 34% of women ages 45–64, and 33% of women ages 65 and older experience high levels of stress. In one week, two out of five women reported a high level of depressive symptoms.

Some identified causes of high levels of depressive symptoms found in women are low income, economic stress, care-giving, lack of social support, physical illness and disability. Fifty-two percent of women earning $16,000 or less and 29% of women earning $50,000 or more suffer high levels of depressive symptoms. Sixty-eight percent of women experiencing economic stress and 32% of women who are not economically bound suffer high levels of depressive symptoms. The responsibility of care-giving uniformly gets passed to women regardless of race, income, or marital status. Care-giving would include the single-parent who single-handedly raises her children and adult children caring for a sick parent or relative. Fifty-one percent of single-parents and 36% of married women with children experience high levels of depressive symptoms. Sixty-eight percent of women who lack social support and 36% of women with support during troubled times suffer high levels of depressive symptoms. Sixty percent women with fair to poor health and 35% women with normal health report a high level of depressive symptoms. Fifty-six percent of women with a disability and 36% of women with no physical limitations show high levels of depressive symptoms.[2]

While women continue their twentieth century struggle for and to prove equality, our health, family and homes are moving in a very different direction. One that signifies that we are not coping, tired, overwhelmed and losing control number one in our own lives and conversely those of our immediate family and home.

Women are turning to various venues for coping with stress. Not only are women finding relief in the growing number of spa and massage salons, but millions of women are addicted to prescription drugs (pain killers and anxiety pills)—the fastest growing addiction in America.[3] Sadly, these findings are not evident in the secular community alone, but experienced amongst the Christian community as well.

The most genuine of Christian women are finding it difficult to manage life, family, and home. Like dieting, women have read numerous books and tried various skill sets for setting order to their lives, family, and home.

The Christian Women's Guide to a Blessed Life book and seminar is a systematic and biblical approach for establishing and maintaining permanent life, family, and home management.

There is life and home management material on the market for the Christian woman that provides success tools for enhancing external productivity and enhancing one's personal relationship with God. Most life, family, and home management books focus on providing the reader with tools that enhance external productivity. While that is a useful approach and being skilled at getting things done easier and faster allots time to do other things, it does not address God's purpose, plan and design for women, nor answer her quest for identity and purpose. It does not guarantee that what that woman is doing is God's will, beneficial, or right. It assumes that we know what is best for our lives and the lives of our family and simply need the appropriate tools for working it out smoothly and effortlessly. While we may give women tools for getting things done, the efforts and direction of that woman may be all wrong leaving her spending time getting things done, but not necessarily the things that are in line with God's will for her. This approach will ultimately lead to and end in frustration.

What makes the Christian Woman's Guide to a Blessed Life unique is that it addresses personal, family, and home management thoroughly and in one volume. The principles taught set the Christian woman on the road of doing God's will by assisting her in setting life priorities that align with His revealed will. Matthew 7:21 states that only those that *do* the will of God will enter the kingdom of heaven, while Matthew 7:24 emphasizes that those who hear and do what Jesus says are wise and by doing so ensure a strong foundation for life. Once the Christian woman understands God's will for her and sets life priorities for fulfilling God's will for her life, family, and home, the Christian Woman's Guide to a Blessed Life then provides its reader with the necessary tools for securing and managing those priorities.

The Christian Woman's Guide to a Blessed Life addresses every area of the woman's life; spiritual, physical, mental, psychological, social and financial; her identity, purpose and self-worth; her dreams, goals and aspirations; her natural abilities, spiritual gifts and learned abilities; and the responsibilities of a family and home. As the reader makes a personal commitment and embraces the principles, the electrifying results are peace with God, the peace of God, completeness, fulfillment, and influence. She becomes a woman of divine purpose and influence, impacting the world around her with God.

Acknowledgements

Lord, thank You for creating and saving me. I am eternally and humbly grateful for the work You've done and continue to do in me. Thank You for the beautiful people You have placed around me and used to effect Your will.

For my husband, Charles M. Neal my teacher, advisor and encourager. Thank you.

For the encouragement of my children, A. Michael, Christopher and Jennifer Neal. Thank you.

For the encouragement from my parents and extended family. Thank you.

For my personal friends who gave me the time and space to develop the manuscript. Thank you.

For the Women of Great Price Discipleship ministry, who at the time released me of my duties, prayed and supported my dream and efforts. Thank you.

For Teresa Cherry, Cheryl Delarge, Monique Rawls, Reverend Clarence and Bridget Taylor, my church cell family and all who whispered a prayer or word of encouragement. Thank You.

For all who helped in the book's production, namely, Sharon Y. Brown, my editor. For her hard work and dedication. For the wisdom and counsel of Annette V. Hampton M.S., MSW, Reverend Harvey Quarles, Reverend Dr. Willie Richardson and Sheila R. Staley M. Ed. Thank you.

Introduction

The *Christian Woman's Guide to a Blessed Life* previously, *Home Management from the Inside Out,* initially debuted in 1993 when I spoke at a women's luncheon on the topic of home and family management. News of its content spread, accompanied by frequent requests for the material. While I accepted the challenge to put the luncheon material in book format, I faced the one question every writer must address, "What makes this material unique?" I found several books on the market that addressed home management. What inspired me to continue writing, however, was what I found as I peered into the homes and listened to the hearts of Christian working women and housewives. The cry was the same and so personally familiar. In spite of all the material written on personal and home management, Christian women, in general, remained overwhelmed, frustrated, even unhappy. My observation told me that as Christian writers (ministers of God's Word), we were not getting to the heart of the problem that weighed down many Christian women in their homes. Had we spent too much time providing "how to's" for enhancing external productivity while neglecting to minister to the primary administrator?

A woman's home and family is an extension of who she is. Was there a single book on the market that addressed family and home management in light of the whole woman, i.e., her mind, body, soul and spirit? Was there a book that spoke to her concerns, aspirations and hardships while directing her towards God's purposes and helping her to know and fulfill God's will?

Believe it or not, the Christian working woman and homemaker share some common concerns related to time management, stamina, tension (stress), temptation, and value. One of her greatest dilemas is how to fulfill her responsibilities while making room for personal time. There never seems to be enough time to satisfy the challenges of the day, complete tasks and secure personal time. If she is not careful, she could spend her time literally running to beat the clock.

Racing against time while attempting to meet the needs, demands and responsibilities of a home and family can make any woman feel she is competing in the decathalon. The typical family life is filled with members of varying personality types and needs, as well as circumstances that do not always comply with the plans for the day. In addition, there may be mental, physical and emotional demands of a job as well as the challenge of turning a deaf ear to the latest philosophies for the modern woman. She retires for the night only to rise to a new day beckoning that if she runs a little harder and perhaps just a little faster, she can complete yesterday's tasks and avoid doing today's work, tomorrow. How does the Christian woman handle the load? Where can she go for solitude?

Tantamount to the vitality of a Christian woman is her value. She asks herself questions like, "Will my husband notice all I did today? After all, despite the disarray of a few things, "little Johnny" (after a full morning of hit and miss) is eating with his spoon." "Will the children realize I put personal hopes and dreams on hold to give them my best?" In the meantime, the world and its applause says her importance lies in her level of education, her job title, how much money she brings to the table, where she lives, what she drives and who her friends and associates are. Will meal preparation, the laundry, house cleaning, teaching the children and lovingly following the leadership of her husband be met with appreciation equal to that of saving a company millions of dollars? Will anyone take note of her and the sacrificial contribution she makes for the family?

Perhaps you have the business of home management down to a science: Jesus, your mate, the kids, the house, and your job. Then one day you wake up, look in the mirror and see yourself for the first time in a long time. You question the identity of the strange woman staring back at you. Is it really you or has the real you gone into hibernation waiting for winter to end and spring to begin? Evaluating the situation, you ask yourself, "How long does this last? How long before I can hold a conversation with someone older than my children? When will I be able to wear a dress to church that remains unwrinkled and unstained? When will eating breakfast consist of something a little more refined than the children's left-overs? When will shopping for me not involve constant stops to the bathroom but rather buying an entire outfit with accessories? When do I and how do I secure time for personal interests?" These and more are the concerns that can toy with our minds, discourage our efforts and cause any Christian woman to question her purpose. This, in turn, affects both family and home.

The goal of the *Christian Woman's Guide to a Blessed Life* is to teach Christian women 1) how to have a blessed personal life while managing their families and homes, 2) how to know and fulfill the will of God by aligning themselves with and obeying Scripture, and 3) how to influence the quality of her family, church, community, and nation's future by doing the revealed will of God.

I have come that they may have life, and have it to the full" (John 10:10b). What an exciting promise from the Lord. Sadly, women live and die never cognitively experiencing the riches of this grace. More disturbing is for a Christian woman to go through life experiencing moments of happiness, but, deep within, living with a broken spirit, a troubled, hurting or lonely heart; and for some, living on the fringes of hopelessness.

18

Most of us, with some exceptions, grew up enjoying a happy childhood. We grew up conditioned to dream of our wedding day, marry prince charming and live "happily ever after." Today, however, instead of the long and flowing white gown, we're up to our knees with dirty clothes, dishes, and the diapers. Do you remember the white runner being rolled out and laced with rose petals? Now we're vacuuming it. Prince charming? Well, he's a little rounder now. And what were once joyful sounds of celebration, have been replaced by the baby's cries and the kids' homework. The throwing of rice is now toys and issues that seem over our head. On a more serious note, marriage, parenting and the finances may not be what you expected. A role reversal is transpiring between you and your parents and signs of your aging are on the horizon.

As sobering as these very real and normal circumstances may be, God's earnest desire is that we have a blessed life in Christ—one characterized by His presence and hand actively governing our affairs as we keep our face before Him. Consequently, even under unfavorable circumstances, our peace remains undisturbed by the calm assurance that God will work it out for our good and for His glory as we submit to Him and meet the conditions set forth in His Word. *The Christian Woman's Guide to a Blessed Life* will provide you with the tools you need for experiencing a blessed personal life.

You are familiar with the phrase, "No man is an island." Who we are, what we do, and what we say affects others. Moreover, as a Christian, we have a biblical responsibility to our neighbor. Through love, God drew us to Himself and redeemed us. As we lift our heads and look around us, we see people in our home, neighborhood, on our job and in our church family with whom we have direct and indirect contact. We may not have the opportunity to make a verbal exchange with each, but who we are, what we say, and what we do directly and indirectly affects others. Some of the conditions in our home, community, job and church will be there until we accept personal responsibility to make a difference by obeying the promptings of the Holy Spirit, being a verbal witness, modeling an exemplary life, and using our natural and spiritual gifts.

God has indwelled the Christian woman for divine purpose and influence. Many women have worked hard and made notable achievements. History records both the negative and positive contributions and influences of these women in our country. To our dismay, we continue to see and live with the effects of atheist, Madalyn Murray O'Hair who led the effort to remove "In God We Trust" from our currency and the 1963 U.S. Supreme Court decision in Murray v. Curlett that ended mandatory prayer and the recitation of Scripture in our public school.[1] Then in 1973 came the U.S. Supreme Court decision to legalize abortion in Roe versus Wade (Jane Roe is now a Christian who publicly speaks against abortion.).[2] To the contrary, are the efforts of women like Marva N. Collins, an educator who began the Westside Preparatory School—a school for poor inner city children of Westside, Chicago—with her pension from fourteen years of teaching in the Chicago public school system[3] and Eliza Shirley, founder of the Salvation Army, and others have also made significant, positive contributions.[4]

As Christian women, we have another legacy. Throughout Scripture we can observe women who exercised great faith and as a result effected significant change. The Old Testament records God calling out a young Jewish girl named Esther. Esther, by God's divine providence, became the queen of Persia. While the enemy of God's people worked hard to destroy them, God had a plan that could not be thwarted. Esther adhered to the counsel of her cousin, Mordecai. She and her maidens fasted and prayed before seeking the king's favor and exposing her ancestral identity. Through obedience and faith, Esther saved her people from annihilation. When we exercise obedience, faith, and love we, too, become Sojourner Truths, lighting the way for the salvation of those near and far.

The *Christian Woman's Guide to a Blessed Life* is designed to equip you with the essentials for being a woman of divine purpose and influence today through personal, family, and home mangement that is biblically based. Its approach is a simple one. Like any well-built structure, a strong foundation is necessary for securing support for the remaining portion of the building. Jesus supports this principle throughout Scripture as we see illustrated in His parable of the wise and foolish builders. "The rain came down, the streams rose, and the winds blew and beat against that house; yet it did not fall, because it had its foundation on the rock" (Matthew 7:25).

Jesus Christ is the foundation for life, securing a strong Christian home, church, and community. God uses the Christian woman to support each. Because the Christian woman is such an intricate part of God's means for blessing the family, church, and community, *The Christian Woman's Guide to a Blessed Life* will lead you on a step-by-step journey with God that will shape your identity, your values, and your purpose, which in turn will shape the direction of your family and home, your ministry in your church body, and your influence on your job and in your community.

Our country is a reflection of the personal beliefs and choices made yesterday. Choices today will determine the nature of its future. Won't you join me in seeking to make a difference through life management that is in line with God's will? Together we can impact the world around us with God.

Your sister in Christ,

[signature]

Barbara,
Keep believing and impacting the world around "you" with God + by your loving heart. I will love + have 12/3/05

22

CHAPTER 1

A Personal Profile

Carrying out the following assignment will give you an overview of your life—a personal profile. By taking a panoramic view at what you do (your choices), you will learn what is important to you and why. Be honest with yourself. Pray and ask the Lord to reveal and confirm what He knows is true about you (Psalm 139:23–24).

WHAT DO YOU BELIEVE?

1. Do you believe that you have the truth in the Gospel?
2. Do you believe that God's Word can do what it declares?
3. Do you desire to be used by God to effect supernatural and lasting change in the lives of

your immediate family members, church and
community?

4. Do you believe Christ is coming back for the
   Church?

You may wonder what these questions have to do
with successful personal and home management. When
we believe that the Bible is the inerrant Word of God, we
understand the unique privilege and wisdom of obeying
it and experience the security (strength and courage)
and freedom it brings. When we believe God's Word has
the power to do just what it says, we will stand firm on
it even if it means we have to stand alone. Being willing to be used by God to make a difference in the lives
of others says that we are personally willing to change
and are receptive to God effecting change in us by
whatever means necessary. These changes ultimately
bring about change in the lives of those around us and
bring glory and honor to God. Lastly, when we keep
Christ's return before us, we know that what we do is
not in vain and what we go through as a result of being
faithful and obedient to God's Word is just for a season
(Romans 8:17). In the end we know that we will receive
the crown of life that God has promised to those who
love Him (James 1:12). Living for the Lord gives us life,
purpose and direction.

WHO OR WHAT IS AT THE HEART OF WHAT YOU DO?

1. Make a list of your responsibilities in the home, on your job, in your church, and in your community.
2. Identify any additional outside circumstances that frequently rob you of time and energy.
3. In light of your list, ask yourself the following questions to determine the motivation for your choices.

Do I have a need to be loved?

Do I live to please?

Is my conversation laced with my accomplishments and achievements?

Do I shower people with gifts rather than allow them to know me?

Do I flatter people?

Will I go to any extreme to get attention (i.e., sickness, working hard for accolades)?

Do I smolder with envy and jealousy?

Do I recognize the daily kind deeds of God toward me?

Is my hunger for outward expressions of love from others ever satisfied?

Am I ultra-sensitive?

Do I have a need to be needed?

Do I volunteer to meet the needs of others, while neglecting my own?

Do I find it difficult to say, "No"?

Do I feel no one can do the job as well as I?

Do I work long and pressing hours believing that if I don't, the work will not get done?

Do I suffer from deep and continual loneliness?

Do I have a need to be accepted?

Do I live to please?

Do I try to impress others with the appearance of a perfect life?

Do I have a fear of telling people what I really think, want, and believe?

Do I fear pursuing reconciliation with persons who have hurt me or vice-versa?

Do I spend money on things I know I really cannot afford?

Do I alter my values, behavior, and choices to match those of the crowd or my circle of friends?

Do I have a need for achievement and success?

Is my life so filled with busy work (at home, church, community, school, or career) that I need to define who I am?

Am I doing things I should be saying "no" to and not doing things I should be saying "yes" to?

Do I see "the project" rather than "the people" working together to accomplish the same goal?

Do I say on a daily basis, "Just one more thing"?

Is my life unbalanced? Do I put off family time or going to the doctor in the interest of one more project?

Am I driven to work beyond health and human limits?

Do I consistently live on five or fewer hours of sleep each night?

Do I have problems sleeping (worry)?

Have I incurred ulcers, high blood pressure, diabetes or heart disease?

Do I have a need to be in control?

Do I long to be in charge and become offended when expected to follow the leadership of others?

Am I outraged when circumstances are not carried out as planned?

Do I become anxious when people do not act the way I think they should?

Am I possessive of family and friends?

Am I frustrated when everything on my "to do" list is not completed?

Do I refuse the genuine help of another because she may not do the job to my satisfaction?

Am I inflexible?

Do I have a problem trusting God and people?

Have I become unmotivated and passive?

Have I given up because the demands are too great?

Do I under-estimate the value of my input?

Have the things I have done gone unacknowledged or unappreciated?

Do I spend most of my day dreaming?

Do I close the shades and prefer living in dark rooms?

Do I spend much of my time watching television, staying in the bed, sleeping, talking on the telephone, or eating?

Do I lack discipline or tend to lose focus?

Am I late meeting responsibilities, deadlines, and appointments?

Do I make false promises to myself such as, "I'll get to it tomorrow?"

Do I allow windows of opportunity to pass by me?

1. Are you doing what you believe God has placed on your heart regarding your home, job, church, and community? If not, why not? Is it related to any of the points mention above? Can it be disobedience? Maybe fear? Finances? Do you need more education? Are you tired or overwhelmed? "For it is God who works in you to will and to act according to his good purpose" (Philippians 2:13). Through the knowledge of His Word, God will bring about conviction in the heart of His children to make a change. You will not have rest

until you address the inner nudging of the Holy Spirit in your heart.

2. Is what you are doing in your home, church, on your job and community what God wants according to His Word? Question #1 carries some precaution. The Bible says that our heart is deceitful above all things and beyond cure. Who can understand it (Jeremiah17:9)? To make decisions on a nudging from the heart alone could prove faulty. "He who trust in himself," another version reads, "in his own heart" is a fool, but he who walks in wisdom is kept safe" (Proverbs 28:26, NAS).

When making decisions regarding what we are to be doing in our homes, on our job, and in our church and community, God will not give direction that will violate some other biblical principle. For example, God would not tell a Christian woman married to an unbelieving husband with two small children, to leave and serve as a missionary in a foreign land. According to God's Word, her home is her mission field. His revealed will is that she teach, train, nurture, and discipline her children and win her unsaved husband to the Lord by being a godly example of the character of Christ (1 Peter 2:21–3:6). If her heart is pulled in the direction of missions, there are other ways she can serve (i.e., writing letters of encouragement, giving a regular financial donation, and prayer). Be sure that your beliefs line up with Scripture before you act (2 Timothy 3:16).

Like any well-run organization, our homes must be well kept and organized to support and service the needs of our family. Husbands need honor, respect, and a loving home for refuge. Infants and children need consistent nurturing, guidance, instruction, and discipline from their parents. God has given women that awesome and challenging task.

God has created us with natural abilities and when we were saved He endowed us with spiritual gifts (Romans 12:4–8; 1 Corinthians 12:4–11 and Ephesians 4:11–12). Our spiritual gifts are for building up the body of Christ (1 Peter 4:10). We experience peace, fulfillment, and satisfaction when we believe and utilize what God has placed in us.

Before stepping out in some direction inside or outside the home, consider timing. The desire you have in your heart may not violate any biblical principle to your knowledge; however, do take a moment to ask yourself, is this the proper time? You may be a working mom who desires to be home. If your husband needs financial assistance to meet the needs of the family, you may need to keep working. You are not violating God's Word. God has designed and commissioned a wife to help her husband (Genesis 2:18). Pray for God to give your husband and you wisdom and guidance for bringing you home.

Conversely, I have seen married women (particularly those with high energy and zeal) with young children fill their lives with work, ministry, organizations, and committees, while either and sometimes all—the children, the home, the mate, and even their own selves—are not properly cared for. I am convinced this is not done purposefully, but that we just don't know. The world is so far removed from the standards for the home from the Bible, that unless we read and study the Word or have someone model or point us to the truths for the family from Scripture, we simply do not know.

While women, wives and mothers need interests outside their responsibilities as a form of expression, personal growth, and development, we ensure proper development and maturity for our family and ourselves when we recognize our season of life and the responsibilities that accompany each. A Christian single adult has freedom to serve in ministry and to pursue various outside interests such as education and travel. The young married woman has freedom to work, serve in ministry and pursue outside interests, with discretion. For the Christian married woman with children, alternatives for actively pursuing and engaging in various outside interests are limited temporarily while raising the children. As the children grow older, opportunities for engaging in sundry forms of outside interest increase. Be patient; being a mother is a demanding on-call ministry; to rush through twenty years of life to get it over with or to relinquish or exchange its responsibility with what may bring instant and personal gratification is to miss a peak period for personal transformation for you and your children. While God uses us to develop our children, He uses them to transform our lives.

When there is a burden on your heart regarding a change of direction you think you should take, pray for God's will in the situation and what He would have you do. Then wait on the Lord for an answer. If you are married, share your concern with your spouse. Get his perspective and ask him to pray for and with you. God will confirm His will for you through His Word. When that occurs, move out in faith and devise a plan for carrying out God's will. God will honor your plan, if it is according to His will, by providing you with the necessary provisions or by giving you the wisdom for increased provisions (Proverbs 16:1–3). Then step out and put the first step of your plan into action. Please remember . . . God will not give you direction or lead you in a path that will violate His Word (His revealed will for you). "The blessing of the LORD brings wealth, and he adds no trouble to it" (Proverbs 10:22).

Moving the Peanut

The process of activating any plan can bring about frustration if you do not understand that more often than not, the plan will not roll over in reality as easily as it did when putting it on paper. There are other components such as other people's wills and schedules, time and opposition that are all a part of what is called, the process. But as my husband always says, "Just keep pushing the peanut."

More than One Coal in the Furnace

When activating any plan inside or outside of the home, seize (take hold of) and exhaust (make the most of) your windows of opportunity. Ecclesiastes 11:6 states, "Sow your seed in the morning, and at evening let not your hands be idle, for you do not know which will succeed, whether this or that, or whether both will do equally well." What lesson should we glean from this passage? Pursue more than one opportunity. Address your opportunities with faith and action. Don't give up. Just keep pushing the peanut.

Expect Opposition

Satan will attack you mentally by getting you to second-guess God's will, God's Word, and yourself. He will attempt to thwart and barricade your progress. Remember, God's promises during these times namely, "You, dear children, are from God and have overcome them, because the one who is in you is greater than the one who is in the world" (1 John 4:4), "No weapon forged against you will prevail" (Isaiah 54:17), and "No, in all these things we are more than conquerors through him who loved us" (Romans 8:37).

If you are unsure about moving out on what is in your heart, get wise counsel from a mature Christian friend. Be careful. Too much outside and unsolicited advice can confuse you or discourage your faith. Always be willing to listen and adhere to the truth.

Through recording your life activities and answering the questions, if you have found that Christ is not at the heart of what you do or that perhaps you are motivated by selfish ambition, living to satisfy others, self-gratification, apathy, or idleness. These are indications that you have become a victim, allowing something or someone apart from God to control and govern your life.

Selfish Ambition

No one would like to think that what she does in her home, on her job, in her community, and particularly for God is rooted by a need to promote herself. We all like to be encouraged. No one likes to feel left out or excluded. However, do you have a deep longing to be recognized, patted on the back and told that you are doing a good job? Do you find that you need constant stroking and that you are motivated only after receiving words of affirmation? Do your dreams and actions die when expressions of love and praise cease? Sometimes this problem is deeply rooted in pride—a strong need to be worshiped and praised. It can also stem from a lack of nurturing or an unmet need for love during childhood. A need for love or acceptance can lead to choices and behavior that promote self. Selfish ambition is sin and if left unaddressed, can have costly results (Galatians 5:19–21; Philippians 1:15–18; 2:3).

If you have a need to be worshiped or praised and it stems from pride, take the time now to acknowledge it to yourself and God (James 3:14–16). He will not condemn you. The Bible says, "For all have sinned and fall short of the glory of God" (Romans 3:23). There is great freedom when we learn to make being honest with ourselves and God a habit no matter how trite or horrible our sin(s) may seem. "He who conceals his sins does not prosper, but whoever confesses and renounces them finds mercy" (Proverbs 28:13). God desires truth in our inner parts (Psalms 51:6). Don't worry what others will think about the changes that you will have to make. Come clean with yourself and with God so that you can experience the peace of God (Isaiah 14:12–17; Proverbs 16:18; 1 Peter 5:6). Remember, all worship belongs to God and Him alone. When we keep that important fact in its proper order, we are at peace with God, others, and ourselves. (For further instruction see chapter nine, The Grace of Humility.)

If your need for recognition stems from an unmet love-need as a child, other people, things, power nor a position can fill your void. Nothing and no one can replace what you have missed. As unfair as it may seem, do not blame anyone. Acknowledge that you did not receive the love you needed or that was due you. Forgive the guilty parties. Then, look to see how God did love you (Psalm 27:10). Often times we dismiss acts of love because the individuals we desired to love us did not render them. Now trust and allow God to heal and fill your heart with Him and prepare you for service.

Living to Satisfy Others

When we live to satisfy other people, we allow someone else to influence our thoughts and decisions. This signifies that we are no longer living for God nor by His principles, but rather for the approval of another human being. People's views become the gauge for our choices. We become deaf to God's personal message through His Word. We elevate the opinions and life experiences of others above God's Word. We pursue and are gratified by the audience of another rather than the presence of God. Our faith is diminished to something or someone we can see. We have sold our heart to another. The Bible calls this idolatry (Exodus 20:3–4).

The Christian woman's sense of completeness can be anchored in no other source apart from what God says is true about her. That has to be enough. You will come to know that it is enough. Listen to this, "But you are a chosen people, a royal priesthood, a holy nation, a people belonging to God, that you may declare the praises of him who called you out of darkness into his wonderful light" (1 Peter 2:9). God says, you are special; that you are accepted, loved and have immeasurable value. The attitude, behavior and choices of a Christian woman whose heart is reserved for and occupied with God, become expressions of the security, freedom, and joy that come from knowing that she is loved unconditionally by Him.

She is free to love God. Her attitude, behavior, and choices become an expression of her love for Him rather than a means of fearfully gaining His approval or the approval of another. She is free to love people and her attitude, behavior, and choices are expressions of love freely given with no thought of it being returned or for self-acceptance. She doesn't have to be concerned with her well running dry, for she knows the One whom she loves will fill it all over again. She is free to enjoy and accept herself because she is loved and accepted by God (John 8:36; Galatians 5:1). Refuse and ignore the temptation to be lured and controlled by anything or anyone apart from God.

Seek to be controlled by God. Allow His Word to govern your life (choices). When we make this our daily prayer, "Lord I give you my life. Order my steps in Your Word and give me the strength to follow You." We can be confident that nothing will come into our lives that has not come past God first and secure enough to know what seems to have passed us by was not meant for us. You can rest assured that the plans He has for you will not harm you, but rather to give you hope and a future (Jeremiah 29:11).

Self-gratification

Living to satisfy self is what the Bible calls vanity and self-gratification (Ephesians 4:17–24; Proverbs 16:1–2; Proverbs 21:2). When speaking of satisfying self, I am not referring to the beauty of knowing you and what you like as an individual such as your favorite color, food, style, or activity. Nor am I minimizing the importance of caring for you. We can mistakenly become enthralled with impressing others, meeting the expectations of someone else or emulating another that we lose sight of who we are and what our needs are (Psalm 139:14). We run into trouble when what we like and desire is contrary to the Word or when gratifying self is more important than pleasing God and serving our fellow man.

At one time, German chocolate cake was my favorite dessert. Early on in our marriage, my husband made one for me every month. I was not satisfied with eating just one slice after dinner. I ate a slice for breakfast, for lunch, and pinched during intervals between breakfast, lunch and dinner. When there was just one piece left, I ate it very slowly hoping to prolong the experience. I shared my cake with much reluctance. Now that's the epitome of self-indulgence (greed) and self-gratification. The Bible says to love God with all of our heart and with all our soul and with all our might and our neighbor as ourselves (Deuteronomy 6:5; Matthew 22:37; Leviticus 19:18).

Apathy

In the story of the Prodigal Son, the older brother was not moved to rejoice with family and friends over his brother's return (Luke 15:25–32). In the same way, Cain was not moved over the murder and loss of his brother, Abel (Genesis 4:6–9). In each case, anger was at the core of each man's apathy. It is not uncommon to hear little children and even adults say, "I don't care." Remember the old adage, "Sticks and stones may break my bones, but words will never harm me."

Both are pride's attempt to shield our true feelings of hurt caused by disappointment or feelings of rejection—as if life's difficulties have no effect on our heart. Disappointment, when left unchecked, can lead to self-pity. When self-pity is permitted to fester, we shun our responsibilities and sensitivity to look on the needs of others. We become self-centered and selfish.

Idleness

Work is not sin. Work was given before the fall and not as a result of the sin of Adam and Eve in the Garden of Eden. Both, the Old and New Testaments declare that if one does not work neither will he eat (Proverbs 19:15; 2 Thessalonians 3:10). God gave Adam the mandate that man should fill and control the earth. Along with responsibility, man was given aptitude, interests, and skill (Daniel 1:7,14). We have a responsibility to God (to worship and serve Him), our neighbor (to serve him or her), and ourselves (to take care of ourselves). To do otherwise would be futile (Genesis 4:1–5).

My youngest son visited West Africa on a short-term mission trip. When we developed the film, he had taken a snapshot of a genuine anthill that was 4 feet tall or better. Proverbs 6:6–11 says, we should go and observe the ant. Although the ant has no chief or ruler over her, she stores (saves) her provisions in the summer when times are well and gathers her food during the harvest when there is plenty. Proverbs 31 says, the virtuous woman set about her work vigorously, that her arms were strong for her tasks and her lamp did not go out at night.

If you tend to be passive, a procrastinator, or doubt your value, refuse to wait for others to motivate you, for a perfect setting, or some emotional stirring. Whether you work inside or outside the home, set and pursue a goal. You will learn in chapter 10 how to set goals that reflect your purpose.

One summer my eldest son was mowing the lawn in our backyard. He noticed bees going into a minute hole. When he brought it to his father's attention, my husband concluded that the bees had built an in-ground nest. By this time there was a swarm of them. When my husband, clothed from head to toe, was able to uncover the unknown, the bees had indeed built a nest the size of a bread plate. He had to set it ablaze several times with gasoline over a 48-hour time span to disband the bees and destroy the nest. (Now there is a spray you can purchase in the home and garden department that will accomplish the same end.). If ants and bees can create, build and store, what about you and me? Start moving with confidence in the love and life God has for you (Hebrews 10:36).

"As a door turns on its hinges, so a sluggard turns on his bed" (Proverbs 26:14). In Proverbs 6, the sluggard is asked how long he will lie down. We all get tired and become disillusioned. Be careful not to fall into the trap that life is a bed of comfort and ease. I noticed my children having a difficult time going back to school on Monday mornings. Then it dawned on me, that during the weekend, they enjoyed sundry forms of fun and relaxation—a far cry from homework and chores they were responsible for during the week. Consequently, they did not want to resume their schedule on Monday. We, too, can have a precarious time resuming our work schedules, particularly when returning from some form of festivity. Getting motivated and avoiding distractions requires discipline, the discipline to do what you know is right regardless of how you feel until you are back into the swing of your routine. Remember that the wages of an idle life is (spiritual, mental, physical, social, and financial) poverty.

Understanding the motivation behind what we do is crucial to our spiritual, physical, and mental well being. Unless God is at the heart of what we do and unless what we do lines up with God's revealed will, which is His Word, we miss experiencing the joy, peace, and contentment of the Lord regardless of the nature of the task (Colossians 3:23–24). Consider the wisdom of Solomon:

> *What does a man get for all the toil and anxious striving with which he labors under the sun? All his days his work is pain and grief; even at night his mind does not rest. This too is meaningless. A man can do nothing better than to eat and drink and find satisfaction in his work. This too, I see, is from the hand of God, for without him, who can eat or*

find enjoyment? To the man who pleases him, God gives wisdom, knowledge and happiness, but to the sinner he gives the task of gathering and storing up wealth to hand it over to the one who pleases God. This too is meaningless, a chasing after the wind (Ecclesiastes 2:22–26).

The woman who lives life apart from God will continually strive, yet remain restless from discontent. The woman who lives in submission to God has a blessed life—not a perfect life and not a life that is without difficulty, but a life filled with the wisdom, knowledge, and contentment that only the Lord can give.

CROSSROADS

"This is what the LORD says: "Stand at the crossroads and look; ask for the ancient paths, ask where the good way is, and walk in it, and you will find rest for your souls. But you said, 'We will not walk in it'"" (Jeremiah 6:16).

We exchange a life rooted in self-centeredness for a life motivated by the love of God when we:

CONFESS: Tell God you are sorry for holding onto the controls of your life (Judges 21:25; Isaiah 64:8–9).

REPENT: Turn from a self-directed life to Christ.

CHANGE: Read and obey Scripture and the leading of the Holy Spirit. Determine to guard against the temptation to make another decision or take another step without clear direction from God (Proverbs 3:5–6; Psalm 37:23; Ephesians 2:10; Philippians 1:6; 2:13; Psalm 1; Joshua 1:8–9; Matthew 7:7–11).

PRAY: Ask the Lord to fashion and set the course of your life according to His will and for His glory (Jeremiah 18:3–6).

TRUST: Believe He will do just what you have asked (Roman 8:28; Hebrews 6:18; Jeremiah 29:11–14; 1 John 1:9).

Daily renew your commitment to do the Lord's will. Depend on Him, just like an infant is reliant upon its mother for its daily care and feeding. Dedicate yourself to a daily intake of Scripture and prayer. Be willing to change and be changed (Isaiah 55:6–11; John 14:26; Hebrews 10:15–16; John 15:5).

After committing to the steps above you can now begin your adventuresome journey in Christ. He promises to never leave you nor forsake you (Hebrews 13:5–6).

THE WORD OF GOD + PERSONAL APPLICATION IN FAITH = SPIRITUAL GROWTH

Spiritual growth + Spiritual growth = Spiritual maturity and Intimacy with Christ

Prayer

Dear Lord, help me to grow so that what I do is from You and for You. Please forgive me for elevating myself and placing others and myself before You. All praise, glory and honor go to You and You alone. Forgive me for wasting my life and time with those things that please me.

Forgive me for not utilizing the aptitude and abilities You have given me to serve You and my neighbor. Lord, I need You to help me to make the necessary changes so that my life pleases You.

When tempted to drown myself in self-pity, cause me to recognize the misfortunes of others, to be thankful and to encourage those whose situations are worse than my own. Lord, I want to make myself available for Your service. No job is too big or too small. Thank You for Your love and forgiveness. In Jesus' name, Amen.

Scenario, "Tried, Tattered, and Torn"

A young wife and mother invites you to her home seeking guidance for knowing God's will for her life.

Looking around you take note that her home is un-kempt. She shares that she is overwhelmed at times. She worries because the children are struggling in school and she can't get dinner served at a reasonable hour. You both sing on the church choir together. The telephone rings and you overhear her disrespectfully telling her husband that she has left his TV dinner in the oven. Rushing to get to choir rehearsal held in the evening on a weekday, she shoves the children in the back seat of the car as she continues sharing the woes of being the president of her children's Parent and Teacher Association and how she believes she should hold Bible study in her home for stay-at-home moms like herself. What counsel would you give your friend?

CHAPTER 2

The Christian Woman's Identity (Ephesians 5:21–31)

⁓

OUR PHYSICAL
IDENTIFICATION

Many things identify who we are. For instance, a birth certificate documents the exact time and location of our birth, our parental descent and physical characteristics such as our nationality, weight, length, the color of our eyes and hair. Our social security number identifies who we are and follows us through life until death. A driver's license or state identification card gives us permission to drive and identifies our state and place of residence. There are other identification markers such as a passport, family tree, family look-alike, and our fingerprint.

Although our physical identity is clearly defined and accounted for, it is possible to go through life not knowing and accepting ourselves. Perhaps you grapple with feelings of inferiority—you question your identity, purpose or value. Quietly, you do not believe you are as gifted, intelligent, or valuable as the next person. Or perhaps you simply need a gentle reminder of the awesome handiwork of God when He fashioned you. I remember visiting my mother's home when I was 21. In the room where I slept was my 8 x 10 graduation picture. I awoke early one morning and as I peered into what was a reflection of me, I wondered who I was and was perplexed over my purpose. Confused at the time, I remembered asking God, "Who am I?"

A WOMAN'S ORIGIN

The Bible is the only accurate source that explains our origin.[1] "God created man in his own image, in the image of God he created him; male and female he created them" (Genesis 1:27). After placing Adam in the Garden of Eden to work and care for it God said, "It is not good for the man to be alone. I will make a helper suitable for him" (Genesis 2:18). God put Adam to sleep and from the rib He took from man, He made woman. By doing so, God created exactly what was fit or appropriate for Adam. God brought the woman to Adam. "The man said, 'This is now bone of my bones and flesh of my flesh; she shall be called woman for she was taken out of man'" (Genesis 2:22–23).

Birth

Conception is the divine work of God. "Now the LORD was gracious to Sarah as he had said, and the LORD did for Sarah what he had promised. Sarah became pregnant and bore a son to Abraham in his old age, at the very time God had promised him" (Genesis 21:1–2). "Isaac prayed to the Lord on behalf of his wife, because she was barren. The Lord answered his prayer, and his wife Rebekah became pregnant" (Genesis 25:21). "When the LORD saw that Leah was not loved, he opened her womb, but Rachel was barren. Leah became pregnant and gave birth to a son . . ." (Genesis 29:31–32). She conceived again . . . . (vs. 33). Again, she conceived . . . . (vs. 34). She conceived again . . . Then she stopped having children (vs. 35).

Jacob slept with Bilhah, Rachel's maidservant. She became pregnant and bore a son to Jacob on Rachel's behalf (Genesis 30:4–5). Bilhah conceived again . . . . (vs. 7). Jacob slept with Zilpah, Leah's maidservant, and bore Jacob a son for Leah (vs. 9–10). Zilpah bore Jacob a second son (vs. 12). Leah bore Jacob a fifth son (vs. 17). Leah conceived again and bore Jacob a sixth son (vs. 19). Some time later she gave birth to a daughter . . . . (vs. 21). God remembered and opened Rachel's womb. She became pregnant and gave birth to a son (vs. 22–23). Some time later Rachel began to give birth to yet another son and had great difficulty. As she breathed her last—for she was dying—she named her son Benoni. But his father named him Benjamin

(Genesis 35:18). Jacob fathered 12 sons and 1 daughter, 13 children in all.

God made each of us unique. "For you created my inmost being; you knit me together in my mother's womb" (Psalm 139:13). "My frame was not hidden from you when I was made in the secret place. When I was woven together in the depths of the earth, your eyes saw my unformed body. All the days ordained for me were written in your book before one of them came to be" (Psalm 139:15–16).

God determined our place and time. "From one man he made every nation of men, that they should inhabit the whole earth; and he determined the times set for them and the exact places where they should live" (Acts 17:26).

Each of us was born with a purpose. "Before I formed you in the womb I knew you, before you were born I set you apart; I appointed you as a prophet to the nations" (Jeremiah 1:5). Abraham became the father of faith, Isaac, the son of promise and the twelve sons of Jacob, the nation of Israel.

You are a gift from God. "Sons are a heritage from the LORD, children a reward from him" (Psalm 127:3). The New American Standard translation of that same passage reads, "Behold, children are a gift of the LORD; The fruit of the womb is a reward." God ordains and utilizes the time of our conception, birth, location, gender, race, family, personality, talents, aptitude, and interests to effect His will.

Your Appointed Time Is No Accident

- Esther came into her royal position at God's appointed time (Esther 4:14).
- But when the time had fully come, God sent his Son . . . (Galatians 4:4).

Your Location Is No Accident

- God placed Adam and Eve in the garden to work and take care of it (Genesis 2:8,15).
- In their efforts to erect the Tower of Babel, God scattered the people over the face of the whole earth (Genesis 11:1–9).
- Jesus' parents resided in Nazareth of Galilee, but Jesus was born in Bethlehem to fulfill prophecy (Luke 2:4,7; Matthew 2:4–6).

Your Gender Is No Accident

- "So God created man in his own image, in the image of God he created him; male and female he created them" (Genesis 1:26–27).

Your Race Is No Accident

- The sons of Noah who came out of the ark were Shem, Ham and Japheth (Ham was the father of Canaan). These were the three sons of Noah, and from them came the people who were scattered over the earth" (Genesis 9:18–19).

Your Family Is No Accident

God's blueprint for the family is for a man and a woman to marry then bear children (Genesis 1:27–28; 4:1–2). If you worry that your family situation is less than God's best, you are not alone. Sarah gave Abraham her maidservant, Hagar, who bore Abraham his son, Ishmael (which was culturally acceptable in the East at that time) (Genesis 16:3–4). Isaac loved his son, Esau and Rebekah, Isaac's wife, loved Jacob, Esau's brother (favoritism) (Genesis 25:28). Rachel and Leah, Rachel's sister, contended over bearing Jacob's children (sister rivalry) (Genesis 30:1–24). Jacob had other children by Rachel's and Leah's maidservants, Bilhah and Zilpah (culturally acceptable in the East at the time) (Genesis 30:3–13). Between Jacob burying Rachel and his father, Isaac, Reuben, his first born slept with his father's concubine, Zilpah (incest) (Genesis 35:22). Joseph brothers sold him into slavery (malice) (Genesis 37:28).

God chose Abraham and promised to make him into a great nation (Genesis 12:1–3). Sarah, Isaac, Rebekah, Jacob, Rachel and Leah were all a part of that plan. God fulfilled his promise to Abraham despite family dysfunction. Through the sons of Jacob, God formed the nation of Israel. In the book of Acts, God saved an entire family by one faithful God-fearing man, Cornelius (Acts 10:1–2, 33,44–48). God knows who you are and where you are. He placed you there. He wants to use you to bring salvation to your home and family.

In addition to the promise God made to Abraham that he would make him into a great nation, God made a covenant with Abraham that he would be the father of many nations (Genesis 17:4–5). Abraham is exactly that. He is the father of faith to all, across the globe and time, who have received the message of salvation by faith. We are Abraham's offspring (Romans 4:9–13; 17–19). We are the family of God.

Your Personality Is No Accident

- Miriam was outgoing, strong, quick and exuberant (Exodus 2:7–8; 15:20–21),
- Ruth was quiet, humble and reserved (Ruth 2:6–7,10,14),
- Esther was purposeful (Esther 4:15–16; 5:1–7; 7:1–6; 8:1–8),
- Mary of Bethany was quiet and pious, while her sister,
- Martha was industrious and hospitable (Luke 10:38–41; John 11–12:1–3)

Your Talent Is No Accident

- Dorcas was known for her artistic ability as a seamstress (Acts 9:36, 39).

Your Aptitude Is No Accident

- Deborah had the ability to handle the office of Judge over the nation of Israel (Judges 4:4–5).

Your Interests Are No Accident

- The virtuous woman was resourceful in balancing family, home, and business (Proverbs 31:16,18,24).

Your personality type, aptitude, interests, and physical features combined define how God made you for accomplishing His will. Live out of who you are—how God made YOU. Your personality, aptitude, talents, interests, physical features, and life experiences are the colors given for your life canvas. There is no one with the exact color blend as you. Use what you have been given to serve God and your neighbor. Fine-tune each through education, reading, meeting with experts in their field, and utilization. In doing so, you will discover other untapped abilities and spiritual gifts. In addition, you will discover God's will and direction for YOU. Obedience to God's revealed will is key. Ruth, Esther, nor Mary, the mother of Jesus, had any idea of the plans God had for them prior to their unfolding. Ruth submitted to the tutelage of Naomi, and Esther submitted to her cousin Mordecdai. Mary lived in a way that found favor with God. Their obedience and submission to God's revealed will for them at the time is what placed them in line to experience God's best.

THE SINFUL NATURE

It is right to be who and what God made us. At the same time we must be aware of the weaknesses of our personality and character, i.e., our sinful nature. "The acts of the sinful nature are obvious: sexual immorality, impurity and debauchery *(indulgence in sensuality)*; idolatry and witchcraft; hatred, discord, jealousy, fits of rage, selfish ambition, dissensions, factions, and envy; drunkenness, orgies, and the like. I warn you, as I did before, that those who live like this will not inherit the kingdom of God" (Galatians 5:19–21, italics mine). Who we are and what we do should not violate the principles of the Bible (2 Corinthians 5:21; 1 Peter 1:14–16).

Put to death, therefore, whatever belongs to your earthly nature: sexual immorality, impurity, lust, evil desires, and greed, which is idolatry. But now you must rid yourselves of all such things as these: anger, rage, malice, slander, and filthy language from your lips. Do not lie to each other, since you have taken off your old self with its practices and have put on the new self, which is being renewed in knowledge in the image of its Creator (Colossians 3:5, 8–10).

Therefore, as God's chosen people, holy and dearly loved, clothe yourselves with compassion, kindness, humility, gentleness and patience. Bear with each other and forgive whatever grievances you may have against one another. Forgive as the Lord forgave you. And over all these virtues put on love, which binds them all together in perfect unity (Colossians 3:12–14).

"But the fruit of the Spirit is love, joy, peace, patience, kindness, goodness, faithfulness, gentleness and self-control. Against such things there is no law" (Galatians 5:23).

The Accuser

As Christians we will contend with our flesh (in my flesh dwells no good thing; Jeremiah 17:9), the lures of the world, and the enemy of our soul, the devil.

We suffer and can never become everything God would have us be when we believe the devil's lies that we are less than what God's Word says we are; when we succumb to fear or cannot get beyond confessed sin; when we fight and hold jealousy and envy against our sisters in Christ rather than appreciating what they bring to our life; and when we are convinced that our value is determined by everything except what God says. Satan is the master mind behind it all. Satan is . . . .

The accuser of the saints (Revelation 12:10).
Our enemy (Genesis 3:1–3; Matthew 13:39).
An evil spirit (1 Samuel 16:14).
The father of lies (John 8:44).
A murderer (John 8:44).

A tempter (Matthew 4:3; 1 Thessalonians 3:5).

The god of this world (2 Corinthians 4:4).

The prince of this world (John 12:31; 14:30; 16:11).

Ruler of the darkness of this world (Ephesians 6:10).

"The weapons we fight with are not the weapons of the world. On the contrary, they have divine power to demolish strongholds. We demolish arguments and every pretension that sets itself up against the knowledge of God, and we take captive every thought to make it obedient to Christ" (2 Corinthians 10:4–5).

"For God did not give us a spirit of timidity, but a spirit of power, of love and of self-discipline" (2 Timothy 1:7).

"But we are not of those who shrink back and are destroyed, but of those who believe and are saved" (Hebrews 10:39).

OUR SPIRITUAL ORIGIN

The Christian woman receives a new identity at the moment of conversion (1 Corinthian 5:17). As a little girl I used to dream of my wedding day. I dreamed of how I would marry prince charming and how he would carry me off into the wonderful land of marital bliss. Everything would be perfect—our marriage and our children. I married a prince and he is indeed charming. When I married my husband, a transaction took place.

I received a new name. My maiden name was dropped, my husband's last name was transferred to me and I assumed a new identity. No longer would I be addressed as Sharie L. Barnes. I became Sharie L. Neal. I assumed my husband's last name and with it a new identity. I would be recognized from now until my life's end as Sharie L. Neal. In addition, everything that belonged to him became ours, his and mine. I received all the rights and privileges to his earnings and property. Although neither my marriage nor my children are perfect, with Jesus at the center, as each of us submits to Him and as the children and I submit to my husband, we are richly and deeply blessed.

Likewise, through salvation a transaction has taken place. We have received a new identity. We (the Church) are the bride of Christ and Christ is our Head.

Jesus Is the Perfect Husband (Ephesians 5:21–31)

According to Ephesians 5:21–31, Paul outlines the practical Christian duties of a husband and wife while metaphorically illustrating the relationship between Christ and the church. In verse 25, Paul tells husbands to love their wives just as Christ loved the church. Verses 25–33 give details of how Christ demonstrated His love for His bride, "the church." It is within these verses that I personally embraced Jesus Christ's love for me. I thought by sharing them with you, you too would know the peace, security and value that comes from knowing you are loved.

Christ loves her (verse 25)

- "I came that they might have life, and might have it abundantly" (John 10:10).
- "Greater love has no one than this, that one lay down his life for his friends" (John 15:13).
- "For one will hardly die for a righteous man; though perhaps for the good man someone would dare even to die. But God demonstrates His own love toward us that while we were yet sinners, Christ died for us" (Romans 5:8–9).

Are you looking for love? Consider Jesus. He took the initiative and was willing to go the distance to secure our love.

Christ gave Himself up for her (verse 25)

- "I am the good shepherd; the good shepherd lays down his life for the sheep" (John 10:11).
- "I lay down my life for the sheep" (John 10:15).
- "No one has taken it away from me, but I lay it down on my own initiative" (John 10:18).

Are you looking for love? Jesus' love is sacrificial.

You are set apart through his death (verse 26)

- "For them I sanctify myself, that they too may be truly sanctified" (John 17:19).
- And so Jesus also suffered outside the city gate to make the people holy through his own blood" (Hebrews 13:12).
- And by that will, we have been made holy through the sacrifice of the body of Jesus Christ once for all" (Hebrews 10:10).

Are you looking for love? Jesus' love is pure. It elevates and makes valuable.

You have been completely washed and cleansed (verse 26)

- "And also some women who had been healed of evil spirits and sicknesses: Mary who was called Magdalene, from whom seven demons had gone out" (Luke 8:2).
- "And such were some of you but you were washed, but you were sanctified, but you were justified in the name of the Lord Jesus Christ, and in the Spirit of our God" (1 Corinthians 6:9–11).
- "But one of the soldiers pierced His side with a spear, and immediately there came out blood and water" (John 19:34).

Are you looking for love? Jesus' love cleanses us from all sin.

You are glorious (verse 27)

- "I praise you because I am fearfully and wonderfully made; your works are wonderful, I know that full well" (Psalm 139:14).
- "All glorious is the princess within her chamber; her gown is interwoven with gold. In embroidered garments she is led to the king; her virgin companions follow her and are brought to you" (Psalm 45:13–14).
- "Fine linen, bright and clean, was given her to wear." "(Fine linen stands for the righteous acts of the saints)" (Revelation 19:8).

Are you looking for love? Jesus' love makes radiant.

You have no spots or wrinkles (verse 27)

- "He who is without sin among you let him be the first to throw a stone at her" (John 8:7).
- ". . . Woman, where are they? Did no one condemn you" (John 8:10)?
- ". . . neither do I condemn you; go your way. From now on sin no more" (John 8:11).
- "Who will bring a charge against God's elect? God is the one who justifies" (Romans 8:33).

Are you looking for love? Jesus' love is free of condemnation.

You are holy and blameless (verse 27)

- "But if he has wronged you in any way, or owes you anything, charge that to my account" (Philemon 1:18).
- "Now where there is forgiveness of these things, there is no longer any offering for sin" (Hebrews 10:18).

Are you looking for love? Jesus' love paid the penalty for sin we owed God and He keeps no record of wrong.

You are nourished and cherished (verse 29)

- "I feel compassion for the multitude because they have remained with me now three days, and have nothing to eat" (Mark 8:2).
- "Children, you do not have any fish, do you" (John 21:5)?
  "Cast the net on the right-hand side of the boat, and you will find a catch" (John 21:6).
  "Come and have breakfast" (John 21:12).
- "Behold I stand at the door and knock, if anyone hears My voice and opens the door, I will come in to him, and will dine with him, and he with me" (Revelation 3:20).

- "But the very hairs of your head are all numbered" (Matthew 10:30).
- "Father, I want those you have given me to be with me where I am, to see my glory, the glory you have given me because you loved me before the creation of the world" (John 17:24).

Are you looking for love? Jesus is giving and caring. His loves fosters companionship.

You are a member of Christ's body (verse 30)

- "But I say to you, I will not drink of this fruit of the vine from now on until that day when I drink it new with you in my Father's kingdom" (Matthew 26:29).

Are you looking for love? Jesus' love fosters intimacy and oneness.

Christ left his earthly mother and heavenly Father for you (verse 31)

- "When Jesus therefore saw his mother, and the disciple whom he loved standing nearby, he said to his mother, "Woman, behold, your son!" (John 19:26).
- "Who, being in very nature God, did not consider equality with God something to be grasped, but made himself nothing, taking the very nature of

a servant, being made in human likeness" (Philippians 2:6–7).

- "And being found in appearance as a man, he humbled himself and became obedient to death even death on a cross" (Philippians 2:8).
- "And about the ninth hour Jesus cried out with a loud voice, saying, 'ELOI, ELOI, LAMA SABACHTHANI? MY GOD, MY GOD, WHY HAST THOU FORSAKEN ME?'" (Matthew 27:46).

Are you looking for love? Jesus' love knows no boundaries. He is totally committed to you and to me. He will fill that empty hole buried deep in your heart. He will satisfy your deepest longing. He is the perfect King, lover, and friend. His love never fails. "The LORD appeared to us in the past, saying: 'I have loved you with an everlasting love; I have drawn you with loving-kindness'" (Jeremiah 31:3).

We become secure and mature Christian women as we submit to Christ and allow ourselves to be loved by Him. We seek love and satisfaction, acceptance and approval in all the wrong places—relationships with people, achievement, and objects. Jesus is the answer to who we are. When the Christian woman takes personal ownership of God's Word regarding her, the pursuit for personal identity, purpose, security, meaning, and worth are satisfied (Galatians 6:3–5). Jesus said that whoever saves his life shall lose it, but whoever loses his life for his (Christ) sake shall find it. When a Christian woman trusts the Lord, she learns that she is complete in Him.

Many Waters Cannot Quench Love

I knew as a parent that I wanted my daughter to trust me. So I consciously chose not to play games with her that would make her doubt my commitment to her. When she was ready to jump off the side of the pool for me to catch her, I could not withdraw my allegiance. I knew that how I treated her would be her example of what she could expect from God. If she could trust that I would not give her a stone for bread, she could trust the Lord. She could believe and accept that what He says about her is true.

One morning during family devotions, she shared what Psalm 139:14 meant to her. She said, "I am special. God loves me just as I am. Even when people think I'm not so pretty (some kids at school did not accept her at the time), I am still acceptable to God."

A Christian woman's relationship with Christ helps her to clearly see both her value and responsibilities. Do not confuse the two. We did nothing to merit our position in Christ. It was a free, but costly gift. Our responsibilities as Christian women are spelled out for us in Scripture. How well we carry out those responsibilities does not alter God's commitment of love toward us. However, it does affect our spiritual growth, effectiveness and rewards. I hope you will concur with my daughter, Jennifer (whose name means gift from God), that you are special and it was all made possible by the love of God expressed through the birth, life, death, and resurrection of our Lord and Savior, Jesus Christ.

PRAYER

Dear Lord, "I praise you because I am fearfully and wonderfully made . . . " (Psalm 139:14). Thank You for creating me, for my uniqueness, for the color of my skin, for my other physical features, for my personality and for my abilities. Thank You for the family you placed me into, by birth and the order of my birth. You did not stop there, but instead placed infinite value on my life enough to die on the cross to relieve me of sin's debt. You saved me and then made provisions for me to live with You throughout all eternity when I die. I thank You for not abandoning me here on earth and for loving me as I am. I did not have to merit your love nor do I have to do anything to keep it. Because of Your love and acceptance of me, I am able to love and accept myself. But even more exciting, Lord, is that I can show and tell others about Your wonderful love and they, too, can have the life I have come to know and the Savior I have come to love. Thank You for giving my life meaning and purpose. ". . . your works are wonderful, I know that full well" (Psalm 139:14).

SCENARIO, "DESSERT"

You are attending a Christian women's conference. When you arrive at the conference site, the lobby is filled with women who share your enthusiasm. Upon entering your room, you meet your assigned roommate. As you both leave for the evening's general session, you vow to come together later that evening for coffee and dessert. Over dessert you share your personal expectations and reasons for attending the conference. Your roommate then discloses that life for her has been like riding on a merry-go-round that won't stop and let her off. Listening, you gather she is a single and successful businesswoman who is angry with God for not having a mate. She is tired of the dating scene and men desiring her for what she seems duty-bound to give. "Everywhere there are demands from the opposite sex, my job, community service I support, and family. Coming to this conference was my only hope for peace of mind." After further inquiry, you learn that she was adopted, followed by the birth of a natural born sibling. In spite of all her accomplishments, her sense of satisfaction is bleak. She feels that no one appreciates her efforts and sacrifices. What words of encouragement can you give her?

CHAPTER 3

Biblical Roles for the Christian Woman

$\mathcal{T}$he Bible gives references to the brawling, discontent, angry, and contentious woman (Proverbs 19:13; 21:9,19; 27:15–16; 30:23). However, her counterpart is God's woman (Proverbs 14:1). God's woman fears God, welcomes God's plan for her life, and lives her life through the provisions God has made for her. God has provided Jesus Christ, His only Son for our eternal security (John 3:16), the Holy Spirit, who is our power and help (John 16:13; Galatians 5:22–26), the Bible which is our power and guide (Matthew 4:4; 2 Timothy 3:16–17), and prayer, our power and peace (Philippians 4: 6–7).

Outlined below are some specific Scriptures that address roles and responsibilities for the Christian woman from the Bible. The material in this chapter has been provided to assist you in knowing God's revealed will for you and to provide you with examples of women who aligned themselves with God's will. What distinguishes these women is their unwavering devotion and reverence for God. Notice their faith, dependence, submission, and obedience to God in their circumstances.

Scriptures That Relate to the Different Roles of Women in the Bible

Being God's woman has not only to do with what she does (her conduct) but her character and the motivation of her heart (Proverbs 27:19; Matthew 7: 21–23; Luke 6:46).

TYPE OF WOMAN	EXAMPLE
The Older Woman (Titus 2:3–4; Ephesians 5:21–33)	Priscilla
TO BE (character): Reverent in the way they live, Not to slander	Acts 18:2,18,26
TO DO (conduct): Not to slander, Not addicted to much wine, Teach what is good, and Train the younger women	
PURPOSE: So no one speaks evil of the Word of God	

The Young Married Woman
(Titus 2:4–5; Ephesians 5:21–33)

Virtuous
Woman

TO BE (character):
Self-controlled, pure,
kind,
Lover of husband and
of children

Proverbs
31:10–31

TO DO (conduct): Busy at home,
Subject to her husband,
Lover of husband, and
Lover of children

PURPOSE: So no one speaks
evil of the Word of God

The Single Woman
(1 Corinthians 7:9,34–35)

Jephthah's
daughter

TO BE (character): Live in a
right way in undivided
devotion to the
Lord

Judges 11:34–40

TO DO (conduct): Marry if
she does not have the gift
of singleness

PURPOSE: To be free from worldly care

The Widow (1 Timothy 5:3–16)

Naomi

Older Widow - over 60, with
children or grandchildren
(Her aid should come from
her children and
grandchildren)

Entire Book of Ruth

WAS (character): To receive
help from the church:
Faithful

WAS (conduct):
Faithful to husband,
Well known for her good
deeds, e.g.,
Bringing up
her children,
Showing hospitality, Washing
feet of the saints,
Helping those in trouble and
Devoting herself to all
kinds of good deeds

PURPOSE: So widows who really
need help can get it

Older Widow - over 60 without   Anna
children or grandchildren

WAS (character): Woman of   Luke 2:36–38
prayer

DID (conduct): Ask God for help
To receive help from
the church:
(See above description)

PURPOSE: No one open to blame

The Young Widow (1 Timothy 5:14)   Ruth

TO DO (conduct): Marry, Have   Entire Book of Ruth
children and
Manage their home

PURPOSE: To give the enemy no
opportunity for slander

The Single Parent
  (By having children outside
  of marriage, death or divorce)

Hagar

TO DO (conduct):
  Work and serve faithfully

Genesis 16:1–16
Genesis 21:8–21

Widow of Zarephath
1 Kings 17: 8–24
Luke 4: 25–26

Women Married to the
  Unsaved (2 Corinthians 6:14;
  1 Corinthians 7:10–16; 1
  Peter 2:19–3:6)

Entire book
of Esther

TO BE (character):
  Reverent and pure,
  Gentle and quiet

TO DO (conduct): Don't be
  unequally yoked,
  Stay with him if he wants to
  be with you,
  Submissive

PURPOSE: To win your
  unsaved mate to
  Christ

PRAYER

Dear Lord, thank You for showing me Your will and my role and responsibilities as a Christian woman. Help me as stated in Romans 12:1–2 to conform my life to Your will. Help me to stay focused and not be swayed by the world. When I am discouraged, help me to remember the blessings of doing Your will. Then allow my life to be an example of Your grace for generations to come.

Scenario, "Please Pass the Roles"

It's a Holiday. The family is gathered together as is its norm. Most of the people in your family are Christians who possess varying levels of commitment and Bible knowledge. The men gather in the family room to watch the football game while the women are in the kitchen cleaning and sipping tea or coffee with dessert. While conversing, the topic of marriage surfaces as you carry on over your cousin Mariam's engagement ring, which she received from the proposal of marriage her fiancé made at dinner. You all gather around her anxious to give her personal advice on what makes a marriage. Aunt Jeanie who still carries the hurt over her twenty-five year marriage that ended in divorce advises Mariam, "Don't give or do everything for him. You won't be respected and he'll just up and leave you." Rich, Great-aunt Janie is married to a successful businessman, and tells Mariam to make sure her fiancé can take care of her. Your single, unsaved Cousin Marlene poignantly suggests if Mariam knows what he is REALLY like. Quickly subverting the last comment, Aunt Penny, married now for thirty-eight years, chimes in telling Mariam, "Men are just big babies, you have to do everything for them." When everyone was finished speaking, silence came over the room as it always did when Grandma Suzie spoke. Gran was a gracious Christian woman who had been married to granddad for 60 years before he died. A woman of few words but words of life indeed. Listening to everyone's advice she opens her Bible (an old and worn one that she kept by her at all times). Gran lives with you and the two of you talk often. You have shared some precious and intimate moments together particularly when you shared with her all you had learned from the Women's Discipleship class held at your church. How do you think Gran will advise cousin Mariam? Is there anything you might add from what you have learned from your women's group?

CHAPTER 4

A Christian Woman's Sexual Conduct

*I*n the previous chapter, we observed Scripture that defined the roles and responsibilities of the Christian woman according to God's will and prevalent in our society. However, there is a practice in our present society that violates Scripture and God's will for women. I am speaking of homosexuality, lesbianism, and bisexuality. The gay community insists and promotes that they are a legitimate however, unique gender. Various circles such as government, the medical community, media, even sections of the church have sanctioned this philosophy. Sadly, individuals have fallen victim to the practice of homosexuality, lesbianism, and bisexuality. In addition to the Christian married and single woman, it is to this woman, I make my appeal.

There is no established description or role in the Bible for the lesbian (a female engaging in sexual intercourse with another female). God calls it a behavior and not a role. God says three things about its practice:

one, that this behavior is repulsive to Him. "If a man lies with a man as one lies with a woman, both of them have done what is detestable. They must be put to death; their blood will be on their own heads" (Leviticus 20:13; 18:29–30), two, it is contrary to His purpose and design for the woman. "Because of this, God gave them over to shameful lusts. Even their women exchanged natural relations for unnatural ones. In the same way the men also abandoned natural relations with women and were inflamed with lust for one another. Men committed indecent acts with other men, and received in themselves the due penalty for their perversion" (Roman 1:26,27; Genesis 2:18,21–25). Lastly, the individual who practices this behavior has no part with God. "Do you not know that the wicked will not inherit the kingdom of God? Do not be deceived: Neither the sexually immoral, nor idolaters, nor adulterers, nor male prostitutes, nor homosexual offenders, nor thieves, nor the greedy, nor drunkards, nor slanderers, nor swindlers will inherit the kingdom of God" (1 Corinthians 6:9–11).

HOMOSEXUALITY, LESBIANISM, AND BISEXUALITY

The practice of homosexuality, lesbianism, and bisexuality violate Scripture two ways. They violate God's blueprint for marriage between a man and a woman. After God created the universe, He created the man, Adam, and from Adam, He formed Eve. He took her to Adam where He united them constituting the first marriage (Genesis 2:22–25). The first marriage God established serves as a model for God's divine will for the institution of marriage and like the creation of the universe, it is fixed.

Scripture states that he made them male, which in Hebrew is zakar, and female, which in Hebrew is negebah: "So God created man in his own image, in the image of God he created him; male (zakar) and female (negebah) he created them" (Genesis 1:27).[1] Genesis 4:24, "For this reason a man will leave his father and mother and be united to his wife, and they will become one flesh," is God's blueprint for marriage. Genesis 4:25 illustrates the blessings of unity and intimacy in a godly marriage. "God blessed them and said to them, 'Be fruitful and increase in number; fill the earth and subdue it'" (Genesis 1:28). All of God's creation has a specific purpose and function. Nothing within God's creation has changed from its original form or purpose. Therefore, any sexual act performed outside of marriage is an act against the will and Word of God, and is, therefore, sin (2 Peter 2:6).

ADULTERY

Adultery is sexual intercourse performed by individuals where one or both are married to someone other than the person they are having sex with. It is the mental, emotional, or physical abandoning of a marriage partner to join or unite with another individual, thus breaking or violating the marriage covenant. Adultery is looking to someone outside of your marriage partner to fulfill your need for love. "You shall not commit adultery" (Exodus 20:14).

"You have heard that it was said, 'do not commit adultery.' But I tell you that anyone who looks at a woman (or man in this case) lustfully has already committed adultery with her (him) in his (her) heart" (Matthew 5:28).

"For out of the heart come evil thoughts, murder, adultery, sexual immorality, theft, false testimony, slander" (Matthew 15:19).

"Marriage should be honored by all, and the marriage bed kept pure, for God will judge the adulterer and all the sexually immoral" (Hebrews 13:4).

Love in Marriage

God's will for a married woman is that she would both give and receive love. "The husband should fulfill his marital duty to his wife, and likewise the wife to her husband. The wife's body does not belong to her alone but also to her husband. In the same way, the husband's body does not belong to him alone but also to his wife" (1 Corinthians 7:3–4). Ladies, intimacy with our husband is meant to be enjoyed. Be aware, however, that there can be various hindrances that work against that end. Addressing them frees us to enjoy what God intended to be a blessing.

Three major areas that confine a Christian woman's freedom for intimacy with her husband are having engaged in sex as a single woman or teen (promiscuity, rape or incest), an inappropriate or unbalanced relationship with her children, and fatigue. The Bible does not lie. When an individual engages in sexual activity, there is not only a physical attachment, but a spiritual, psychological, and emotional one as well. "Do you not know that he who unites himself with a prostitute is one with her in body? For it is said, 'The two will become one flesh'" (1 Corinthians 6:16). In simpler terms, something happens internally that cannot be easily undone. If a woman has had more than one sexual partner, the problem becomes compounded. Having had one or more sexual partners prior to marriage may cause a woman to experience dissatisfaction or a lack of sexual fulfillment with her husband. She may have difficulty experiencing feeling from the heart. Depending on how she has mentally and emotionally handled those relationships could alter her personality and the condition of her heart. If she has been a victim of rape or incest, she may experience inhibitions or sensitivity to certain touches. If you are a victim of sexual abuse or have engaged in numerous sexual relationships outside marriage and if you are experiencing any of the symptoms discussed, God's desire is to see you made whole again. Pray and ask the Lord to give you the courage and wisdom for addressing this area of your life. Whatever you do, do not continue to hide or mask yourself behind it. For you, your mate, and your marriage, seek help from a good Bible counselor or Bible counseling center. You want to be liberated and healed to experience God's best.

A good mother will love her children, but it is not God's will that our children fill a place or love need that God intended that only our husband should meet. We cannot allow our young children to sleep in bed with our husband and us. This is a new and growing trend that is due to, according to Dr. T. Berry Brazelton, parent's work schedules and the desire to spend quality time with an infant or small child. He adds that it can come about due to problems a child may have sleeping throughout the night or a mother's desire to be close to her infant.[2] Prolonged co-sleeping arrangements is not good for the child nor is it good for our marriage. It is not conducive for spontaneous intimacy between a husband and wife nor does the child learn respect for the husband-wife union. According to Dr. Brazelton, the child becomes dependent on his parent's presence for falling asleep in return making it difficult for him to learn to put himself to sleep and stay asleep during light-deep sleep cycles. An infant should be weaned to his or her own bed upon arriving home from the hospital. They are in their own crib while they are in the hospital. It starts subtly. Because we're tired, we feed them in bed with us during late night or early morning feedings, where both mom and baby fall asleep. The baby becomes accustomed to these conditions. When we place "little Johnny" in his bed now, he screams. Being a caring mother, we reason with their pain and anguish and before long, what began as a simple fix has become a big problem, particularly for our husband, our marriage, and us. We do not always recognize it initially, then when we do, sometimes we justify it. Seek out an older experienced Christian woman and allow her to teach you how to get your little one out of your marriage bed and marital intimacy back in. You can also refer to "Sleep: the Brazelton Way" by T. Berry Brazelton M.D. and Joshua D. Sparrow, M.D.

Whether you are a stay-at-home-mom or work outside of the home, the work, needs, homework, and appointments are often endless. Remember your priorities—not just what is important, but rather what is *most* important. Secondly, remember to maintain balance. We need our husband's touch for fulfillment and healing. He needs our touch, a touch that only we can give. Take the time to plan an enjoyable evening with your husband. Other things may very well be pulling at you, but for one night a week, have the children do their homework early. They can have soup and sandwiches or pizza and chips for dinner that night. They will survive.

Get an older Christian woman from your church or a mature Christian teenager to watch your children for the evening. Do not leave young children or teens home alone nor unsupervised. Get your husband involved in the process by telling him your desire to be with him, but you need his help. Let him choose between the dishes or homework with the children. Start the ball rolling the day of by calling him at work and coaxing him to envision the evening. As a married woman, it's okay to make the first move sometimes. Both of you should pray for your evening together. Pray together at the start of the day and individually throughout the day, against any interference for a blessed evening. Refuse to succumb to any darts Satan may throw your way to cause friction between your husband and you that day and evening. Satan will attempt to thwart your plans. He is anti-family.

It is not in God's will for a Christian woman to deprive her husband of sex for no good reason. "Do not deprive each other except by mutual consent and for a time, so that you may devote yourselves to prayer. Then come together again so that Satan will not tempt you because of your lack of self-control" (1 Corinthians 7:5). There are two reasons the Bible permits refraining from sex in marriage: for a period of prayer (1 Corinthians 7:5) and if a woman is menstruating (Leviticus 18:19).

Anger is not a legitimate reason for a Christian woman to withhold sex from her husband. Let us take a look at Scripture, "In your anger do not sin. Do not let the sun go down while you are still angry, and do not give the devil a foothold" (Ephesians 4:26–27). Let me say and listen to me carefully: if your mate offends you, lovingly and humbly tell him his fault. First, pray for the right perspective, a godly attitude and for the right time to share the offense. If you are prone to outbursts of rage, it may take a few days before you can present your offense in a way that would be pleasing to the Lord.

Be determined to present your offense in a godly manner. Refuse to give way to your initial emotions.

Refuse to seethe with anger, hold a grudge, or rehearse the offense in your mind. Submit to God no matter how little, big or painful the offense may be. Be willing to submit to Scripture regarding showing your husband respect. Take the offense to the Lord and ask Him to give you the right perspective. Be willing to accept God's perspective on the situation above your own.

Be willing to acknowledge personal failures to God and yourself. Ask God for forgiveness. Now, be willing to forgive your husband with the same forgiveness you have just received from the Lord. Forgive your husband before the Lord prior to even going to him, even before he becomes aware that he has offended you. You may find that it is settled there and that there is no reason to inform him of his offense—particularly if it is a random offense. If your husband's offense is repetitive, go to him, but again, pray for the right time and how to best present the matter. Also, place it on the running prayer list you have for your husband. Pray for your husband consistently and fervently. God will bring about the circumstances that will work necessary change in his life. God's desire for you and me is that we collaborate with Him. God can bring about change in a man without breaking him, but if He chooses to do so, God uses the Christian wife to love and encourage him along the way. This is a ministry whereby we cannot harbor anger, bitterness, or resentment, but rather extend patience, mercy, and grace.

Some marital conflicts take time to resolve. Do not be offended by what appears to be a lack of sensitivity from your husband when he desires intimacy, despite conflict. Men and women are different. Most men can be intimate despite an offense. Intimacy for most men is primarily physical, whereas for a woman it is both physical and emotional. A conflict will not deter our husband's desire for us physically. For some, intimacy is a legitimate resolution to conflict (although it is not).

Be particularly careful when faced with your husband's desire for intimacy when you are melancholy due to marital conflict. Refrain from fulfilling your biblical responsibility out of duty alone. While a Christian women must be willing to give her body freely to her husband, it is not healthy for you or your marriage to perform sex out of duty. Whatever the issues are in your marriage, follow the aforementioned process. When your husband desires intimacy and you find yourself gloomy, excuse yourself for a moment. Then go to the bathroom to get dolled up. While there, tell God where you are. Release your feelings and concerns completely to Him. Let God know that you are placing your feeling and concerns in His hands and will trust Him with your cares as you submit to Him and love your husband. Then move forward as a woman of faith and love your husband through the power of the Holy Spirit. He will be blessed, you will be blessed and God will be glorified. These small steps will keep you from a bitter and callous heart.

A Christian woman's responsibilities and the nature of her menstrual cycle can bring about periods of fatigue. To muster up enough energy to love your husband can appear overwhelming. If fatigue persists as a way of life, evaluate your priorities. Perhaps you need to simplify your expectations, then modify your tasks. Delegate responsibility to family members. Scheduling a visit to your primary care physician for a physical exam may be in order.

Go back to basics. The basics in our lives are the foundations on which our life functions at its best, i.e., our relationship with God, respect for our husband, the teaching, training, nurturing and disciplining of the children, proper rest, at least ten minutes of exercise each day, and a healthy diet. Then gradually add, in order of importance, those things you must do—the things neither you nor your family can live without and that no one else can do (work outside the home, dinner, the wash, finances). For everything else, such as outside activities, consider your season of life. Perhaps this is not the time to take on anymore. For additional household duties, have the rest of the family help you. The key to intimacy with our husbands is to take responsibility to love them, allow and accept the love they know and have to give, address conflict, keep our lives balanced, and submit to God.

HOMOSEXUALITY, LESBIANISM AND BISEXUALITY

Homosexuality, lesbianism, and bisexuality violate God's standard for abstinence from sex until marriage. God is the Creator of the human race (Genesis 1:27).

He established the institution of marriage for companionship and procreation (Genesis 1:28, 22–25). Sex was designed by God to be enjoyed in marriage for intimacy and procreation. "The man and his wife were both naked, and they felt no shame" (Genesis 2:25). "Adam lay with his wife Eve, and she became pregnant and gave birth to Cain" (Genesis 4:1). From the beginning of time to the present, nothing God has created has abdicated its purpose for which God created it. Sex is a gift from God to be exercised in marriage between a man and a woman.

FORNICATION

Fornication is sexual intercourse performed by unmarried and married persons. Fornication is illicit sex. Illicit sex is a violation against God, your body, and your spirit. Fornication is sexually immoral.

"Flee from sexual immorality. All other sins a man commits are outside his body, but he who sins sexually sins against his own body" (1 Corinthians 6:18).

"We should not commit sexual immorality, as some of them did—and in one day twenty-three thousand of them died" (1 Corinthians 10:8).

"The acts of the sinful nature are obvious: sexual immorality, impurity and debauchery, idolatry and witchcraft; hatred, discord, jealousy, fits of rage, selfish ambition, dissensions, factions and envy, drunkenness, orgies, and the like. I warn you, as I did before, that those who live like this will not inherit the kingdom of God" (Galatians 5:19–21).

PROSTITUTION

Prostitution is the practice of giving over one's body to perform and provide sexual favors in exchange for money. "Do you not know that he who unites himself with a prostitute is one with her in body? For it is said, 'The two will become one flesh.' But he who unites himself with the Lord is one with him in spirit" (1 Corinthians 6:16–17).

There is a story that is recorded in the book of Ezekiel about two sisters who became prostitutes in their youth. The story the LORD relates characterizes the behavior of Samaria and Jerusalem, but is one that bears our attention:

The word of the LORD came to me; Son of man, there were two women, daughters of the same mother. They became prostitutes in Egypt, engaging in prostitution from their youth. In that land their breasts were fondled and their virgin bosoms caressed. The older was named Oholah, and her sister was Oholibah. They were mine and gave birth to sons and daughters. Oholah is Samaria, and Oholibah is Jerusalem. Oholah engaged in prostitution while she was still mine; and she lusted after her lovers, the Assyrians-warriors clothed in blue, governors and commanders, all of them handsome young men, and mounted horsemen. She gave herself as a prostitute to all the elite of the Assyrians and defiled herself with all the idols of everyone she lusted after. She did not give up the prostitution she began in

Egypt, when during her youth men slept with her, caressed her virgin bosom and poured out their lust upon her. Therefore I handed her over to her lovers, the Assyrians, for whom she lusted. They stripped her naked, took away her sons and daughters and killed her with the sword. She became a byword among women, and punishment was inflicted on her. Her sister Oholibah saw this, yet in her lust and prostitution she was more depraved than her sister. She too lusted after the Assyrians-governors and commanders, warriors in full dress, mounted horsemen, all handsome young men. I saw that she too defiled herself; both of them went the same way. But she carried her prostitution still further. She saw men portrayed on a wall, figures of Chaldeans portrayed in red, with belts around their waists and flowing turbans on their heads, all of them looked like Babylonian chariot officers, natives of Chaldea. As soon as she saw them, she lusted after them and sent messengers to them in Chaldea. Then the Babylonians came to her, to the bed of love, and in their lust they defiled her. After she had been defiled by them, she turned away from them in disgust. When she carried on her prostitution openly and exposed her nakedness, I turned away from her in disgust, just as I had turned away from her sister. Yet she became more and more promiscuous as she recalled the days of her youth, when she was a prostitute in Egypt. There she lusted after her lovers, whose genitals were like those of donkeys and whose emission was like that of horses. So you longed for the lewdness of your youth, when in Egypt your bosom was *caressed and your young breasts fondled. Therefore, Oholibah, this is what the Sovereign LORD says; I will stir up your lovers against you, those you turned away from in disgust, and I will bring them against you from every side ."So I will put a stop to the lewdness and prostitution you began in Egypt. You will not look on these things with longing or remember Egypt anymore. So I will put an end to lewdness in the land, that all women may take warning and not imitate you (Ezekiel 23:1–22,27,48).*

God's will for single women is to remain pure, a virgin. Today sexual immorality (fornication) is running rampant. Any behavior or sin that grieves the heart of God will surely invoke His wrath. God's Word stands. It should be the utmost priority of every Christian mother to teach and train her daughter—and the determination of every Christian single woman—to be holy. As Christian women we must take hold of the challenge to honor the Lord, to model and emanate propriety in the midst of a world that has lost sight of God.

- You do not have to be mastered by anything (1 Corinthians 6:12)
- Remember you are the Lord's (1 Corinthians 6:17) - Salvation
- The LORD is your husband (Isaiah 54:5)

As in anything sanctified by God,

- Be devoted to the Lord in body and spirit (1 Corinthians 7:34) - Sanctification

- Be concerned about the Lord's affairs (7:34) - Service
- Honor the Lord with your body (1 Corinthians 6:20)

So I tell you this, and insist on it in the Lord, that you must no longer live as the Gentiles do, in the futility of their thinking. They are darkened in their understanding and separated from the life of God because of the ignorance that is in them due to the hardening of their hearts. Having lost all sensitivity, they have given themselves over to sensuality so as to indulge in every kind of impurity, with a continual lust for more. You, however, did not come to know Christ that way. Surely you heard of him and were taught in him in accordance with the truth that is in Jesus. You were taught, with regard to your former way of life, to put off your old self, which is being corrupted by its deceitful desires; to be made new in the attitude of your minds; and to put on the new self, created to be like God in true righteousness and holiness (Ephesians 4:17–24).

HOMOSEXUALITY, LESBIANISM, AND BISEXUALITY

Homosexuality or lesbianism is called sodomy in the Bible. Sodomy is sin and therefore judged by God in Scripture. Genesis chapter 18 records the destruction of the city of Sodom and Gommorah because of their sexual immorality and perversion. The Bible says the outcry against Sodom and Gomorrah was so great and their sin so grievous that the LORD went down to see if what they had done was as bad as the outcry. God destroyed Sodom and Gomorrah by raining down burning sulfur. "Do you not know that the wicked will not inherit the kingdom of God? Do not be deceived: Neither the sexually immoral, nor idolaters, nor adulterers, nor male prostitutes, nor homosexual offenders, nor thieves, nor the greedy, nor drunkards, nor slanderers, nor swindlers will inherit the kingdom of God" (1 Corinthians 6:9–10).

Sin has a way of placing a burden of heaviness on us. However, when exposed to the Light, that burden is transformed into sweet relief and rest. Look at verse eleven of the same passage, "And that is what some of you were. But you were washed, you were sanctified, you were justified in the name of the Lord Jesus Christ and by the Spirit of our God." In Matthew 11:28, Jesus beckons those weary and burdened to come to Him, to escape the burden of living independent and alone for a life accompanied with Him and the love He has to give. He adds in Hebrews 10:17–18, ""Their sins and lawless acts I will remember no more." And where these have been forgiven, there is no longer any sacrifice for sin."

Most women who struggle with any form of sexual perversion are victims. Perhaps you were exposed through sexual molestation as a child by a family member or close family friend. Perhaps you were exposed to perverted sex through the media such as video movies, cable television, magazines, music or books. (We need to be aware and ultra-sensitive to what and to whom our children are exposed. No child should be exposed to any environment where there is kissing, caressing or hugging outside of a Christian connotation.) You may have struggled between the guilt and the pain of being violated yet at the same time aroused and stimulated by the memory of its tantalizing sensation. You may have become a victim through ignorance and unsupervised play with other children. You may have been trying to fill an unmet need for love that should have been provided by your parents, particularly your father.

Coming to God with the sin of sexual perversion may seem difficult or hopeless. It may seem easier to remain in sin than to face feelings of guilt, worthlessness, or shame before a holy God. But God loves you. Absolutely nothing can separate us from the love of God that is found in Jesus Christ (Romans 8:38–39).

There is a way of escape. So, don't give up even though many of your attempts to stop sinning have ended unsuccessfully. The Bible says, "For all have sinned and fall short of the glory of God" (Romans 3:23). You can ask any sincere Christian and they will tell you, we all have needed God's forgiveness. Not one of us was righteous. It was the burden of our helplessness and unrighteousness that let us know we needed (and still need) God. According to John 3:16–17, God loves mankind and has made provision for man's sins through Christ. If you engage in any form of sexual sin your lifestyle is not acceptable to God. Sex was created to be shared within the confines of marriage. Neither is it God's will that we marry or abide with the same sex.

God extends forgiveness and grace to anyone willing to turn from their sin to Christ.

"The Lord is not slow in keeping his promise, as some understand slowness. He is patient with you, not wanting anyone to perish, but everyone to come to repentance" (1 Peter 3:9). "But God demonstrates his own love for us in this: While we were still sinners, Christ died for us" (Romans 5:8).

> *For God so loved the world that He gave His one and only Son, that whoever believes in him shall not perish but have eternal life. For God did not send his Son into the world to condemn the world, but to save the world through him. Whoever believes in him is not condemned, but whoever does not believe stands condemned already because he has not believed in the name of God's one and only Son. This is the verdict: Light has come into the world, but men loved darkness instead of light because their deeds were evil. Everyone who does evil hates the light, and will not come into the light for fear that his deeds will be exposed. But whoever lives by the truth comes into the light, so that it may be seen plainly that what he has done has been done through God (John 3: 16–21).*

Jesus Christ is the solution. He loves you. He died on the cross to pay your sin debt and mine. Now He awaits with open arms and an open heart for you to come to Him. He forgives and wants to save you. All you have to do is acknowledge your sin (that God is right and you are wrong) to a Holy God and be willing to turn from sin to Christ for forgiveness and salvation. I say "willing" to forsake your ways because we cannot forsake sin on our own. It takes the power of God that only Christ can give to forsake sin and be healed. But if you are willing, He will meet you right where you are and help you. "But just as he who called you is holy, so be holy in all you do; for it is written: 'Be holy, because I am holy'" (1 Peter 1:15–16).

"If we confess our sins, he is faithful and just and will forgive us our sins and purify us from all unrighteousness" (1 John 1:9).

"As the Scripture says, 'Anyone who trusts in him will never be put to shame.' For, everyone who calls on the name of the Lord will be saved" (Romans 10:11,13).

If you want to be set free from a life of sexual immorality, pray this prayer. If you mean it from your heart, God will hear you, forgive you and give you a new beginning.

Prayer

Dear Lord, according to Your Word, I have sinned against You greatly. I am sorry for my sin. I want to turn from my sin. Please forgive me for all the wrong I have done. Deliver me from this evil and the Evil One. Wash me, cleanse me and make me whole. Give me a new mind and a new heart to live for You. Give me the power to forsake my old ways and companions. Help me to embrace my new life and to never turn back. In Jesus' name I pray. Amen.

A New Life

Welcome to your new life in Christ! Scripture says, "Therefore, if anyone is in Christ, he is a new creation; the old has gone, the new has come" (1 Corinthians 5:17). The next steps are important. Pray and ask God to lead you to a Bible believing and teaching church. Become a part of the fellowship and attend the Bible Study class regularly, purchase a New International Version Bible, and read your Bible daily beginning with the book of Ephesians in the New Testament. For extra reading, purchase *"Pilgrim's Progress"* by John Bunyan or *"Hinds Feet in High Places"* by Hannah Hurnard. These books will encourage you on your new journey.

Another step you may consider taking is breaking old ties with no explanation. Don't try to explain at this time. Get out of the relationship or situation with haste if possible. If necessary, write a letter with no return address. Settle any financial obligations. What you don't need is any coercion to draw you back into the life you have left. You may need to move back home with your parents, a sibling, or someone you know who will hold you accountable for your new life. If needful, get medical help and or counseling from a Bible-centered Christian counseling center or Christian psychologist. Avoid secular counseling or any counseling where the Word of God is not honored and taken to heart.

PRAYER

Dear Lord,

You have prescribed Your will for the single and married woman. Your desire is that we be holy. I do not pray for myself alone, but for all Christian women. Help Christian single women to be strong, to honor their marriage to You and to not commit adultery against You. May they remain faithful and pure in their marriage to You and seek to please You as a Christian wife would her husband.

Help Christian wives to respect their husbands and be willing to receive love from them. May they keep their priorities in line with Your will, in order to maintain balance and lovingly address conflicts. Help Christian women to be the salt of the earth and the light of the world in the way they honor You with their bodies and in their marriages.

Commitment of purity for the single woman:

Single women whether you have committed sexual sin or have remained pure, do you promise from this point on to accept the Lord as your husband and to give yourself wholly to Him, to not be mastered by anyone, but to be one with Him alone? Will you be devoted to the Lord in body and spirit? Will you concern yourself with the things that concern Him? Do you promise to commit your body wholly to Jesus Christ and to remain pure until marriage? If you have read and solemnly considered what God requires of every woman and you agree to comply with the terms of God's will, say, "I will" and sign this agreement between you and God.

NAME_____ DATE_____

Commitment to holiness for the married woman:

Do you promise to honor the Lord by respecting your husband in spirit, word and deed? Will you be faithful, keeping yourself mentally, emotionally, and physically for him alone? Will you love him and receive the love he desires to give? Will you keep your priorities in line with God and His will for marriage? Will you maintain balance so as to ensure time and devotion to your husband? Will you address conflict in a loving and respectful manner? If you have read and solemnly considered what God requires of every Christian wife and you agree to comply to the terms of God's will, say, "I will" and sign this agreement between you and God.

NAME_____ DATE_____

Commitment to godliness for the Christian woman

A Christian woman is a woman of divine purpose and influence. We have the power to impact the world around us with God. In order to do so, there are some terms we need to agree upon. Will you honor the Lord with your body in spirit, form, and fashion? Will you uphold the honor of a Christian woman and lovingly encourage, even challenge your sisters in the Lord to the same? Will you take responsibility to be a role model, teacher, and encourager for the generation of young women coming behind you? Will you take responsibility with your sisters in Christ to do your part to emanate God's will before women who are unsaved and seize every opportunity to show them the way to a blessed life in Jesus Christ? If you have read and solemnly considered God's will for the Christian woman and you agree to comply to God's will, say, "I will" and sign this agreement between you, your sisters in Christ, and God.

NAME_____ DATE_____

SCENARIO, "TOTALLY COMMITTED"

You conduct a women's Bible study and have just completed teaching this lesson. After the crowd disperses, a young, Christian, married woman approaches you and shares that she loves her husband but is not being sexually fulfilled in her marriage. She confesses that sometimes she feels a strong urge to resort to other means. As you probe, you learn that she was sexually abused repeatedly as a child and grew up in a home where she was exposed to pornography through graphic posters and sexually illicit books. When asked if there was anything else, she shamefully shared how guilty she felt over the inappropriate manner she and some of the girls in her neighborhood played house. Feeling relieved by sharing the information with someone she trusted and respected, she confessed that she knew she had a problem. She wanted to do what pleased God, but how could she rid being haunted by the behavior of her past. What counsel would you give this young Christian wife and mother?

CHAPTER 5

The Virtuous Woman—A Biblical Role Model (Proverbs 31:10–31)

A wife of noble character who can find? She is worth far more than rubies. Her husband has full confidence in her and lacks nothing of value. She brings him good, not harm, all the days of her life. She selects wool and flax and works with eager hands. She is like the merchant ships, bringing her food from afar. She gets up while it is still dark; she provides food for her family and portions for her servant girls. She considers a field and buys it; out of her earnings she plants a vineyard. She sets about her work vigorously, her arms are strong for her tasks. She sees that her trading is profitable and her lamp does not go out at night. In her hand she holds the distaff and grasps the spindle with her fingers. She opens her arms to the poor and extends her hands to the needy. When it snows, she has no fear for her household; for all of them are clothed in fine linen and purple. Her husband is respected at the city gate, where he takes his seat among the elders of the land. She makes linen garments and sells them, and supplies the merchants with sashes. She is clothed with strength and dignity; she can laugh at the days to come. She speaks with wisdom, and faithful instruction is on her tongue. She watches over the affairs of her household and does not eat the bread of idleness. Her children arise and call her blessed; her husband also, and he praises her :"Many women do noble things, but you surpass them all." Charm is deceptive, and beauty is fleeting; but a woman who fears the Lord is to be praised. Give her the reward she has earned, and let her works bring her praise at the city gate (Proverbs 31:10–31).

wife of noble character who can find? She is worth far more than rubies (verse 10). Noble can be characterized as strength, capability, skill, valor or wealth. "Many women do noble things, but you surpass them all" (verse 29). This remarkable woman personifies the essence of, *"The Christian Woman's Guide to a Blessed Life."* What makes the Proverbs 31 woman so extraordinary? Let us take a closer look.

The Virtuous Woman—A Biblical Role Model
(Proverbs 31:10–31)

A Closer Look at the Virtuous Woman

WHO SHE WAS . . . (CHARACTER)	*WHAT SHE DID . . .* (CONDUCT)
vs. 10 - Strong in character	vs. 13 - She worked with willing hands
vs. 11 - Faithful	vs. 14 - She went where necessary to get the best
vs. 12 - Filled with goodness	vs. 15 - She cooked breakfast
vs. 15 - Obliging	vs. 17 - She worked within the boundaries of her abilities
vs. 16 - Resourceful	vs. 19 - She sewed
vs. 17 - Positive and vibrant	vs. 20 - She helped the needy
vs. 18 - Thinker, planner, diligent	
vs. 20 - Charitable and compassionate	
vs. 21, 27 - Committed to her family	vs. 21 - She took good care of her family—their physical and emotional needs
vs. 22 - Committed to her spouse and their intimacy	vs. 22 - Decorator and stylish

vs. 22 - Committed to herself, carries herself with dignity	vs. 22 - Took care of herself
vs. 23 - Wise mate selector	vs. 23 - Chose a respectable mate for a husband and father
vs. 25 - Spiritual and stable	vs. 24 - Kind business woman
vs. 26 - Wise, faithful and true	vs. 26 - Spoke with wisdom and was a kind teacher
vs. 28,31 - Worthy of praise	vs. 27 - Homemaker, diligent, and busy
vs. 29 - Woman of excellence	vs. 29 - Hard worker
vs. 30 - Devoted to serving the Lord	vs. 30 - Motivated by the Lord and all she did was unto the Lord
vs. 31 - Faithful steward	vs. 31 - Rewarded by the fruit of her hands

Out of this woman's reverence for the LORD, she brought to the table of her marriage and family spiritual, physical, emotional, and financial sustenance. The key to a Christian woman's pursuit of excellence lies embedded in her reverence for the LORD. It is honor and reverence for the LORD that molds character and shapes a family.

Being a good personal and home manager does not lie solely in technical skill, but more on a Christian woman's personal relationship with Jesus Christ. Jesus' presence in her life gives her wisdom, power and direction for her life and the life of her family. Proverbs 1:7 says, "The fear of the LORD is the beginning of knowledge, but fools despise wisdom and discipline." Both godly wisdom and discipline characterize the virtuous woman's life. It is her reverence for God that shapes her character, conversation, and conduct.

I have a friend who has the gift of wisdom. The women in our congregation love to sit under her teaching. Once, when I visited her home, she took me to the upper level and led me to a special room. When one of her sons moved out, she had set this room aside (sanctified) as a special place where she and the Lord would meet each morning. And if that was not enough, every year she asked the Lord for a theme. That particular year the theme was, "Lord, Fill My Cup." No doubt, the wisdom she possesses is born out of an earnest commitment to honor the Lord.

"Charm is deceptive, and beauty is fleeting; but a woman who fears the LORD is to be praised" (verse 30). The media, up-scale department and health stores, spas, hair and nail salons spend a fortune vying for our attention and financial resources. We in turn give it to them because we enjoy looking good. When we look beautiful, we feel good about ourselves. While looking our best is important and fun, it does not last. Even our bodies undergo change, no matter how much we walk or how much cream we apply. It is what is on the inside that counts. Isn't it amazing that no amount of clothing, jewels, perfume or etiquette, regardless of how they make us look or feel, compares to coming across the path of a woman who loves the Lord and whose life and family reflect her faith. She is sure yet humble and strong yet meek, steadfast and yet loving. We never want to leave her presence. We want to glean lessons from her and let whatever she has rub off on us.

Proverbs 12:4 states that, "A wife of noble character is her husband's crown, but a disgraceful wife is like decay in his bones." A disgraceful wife will bring disappointment; she shatters human emotions, causes disillusionment and can break her husband's spirit. Conversely, the virtuous woman brings happiness to her husband all the days of his life (verse 12). She does not make his life unpleasant or difficult. Proverbs 31:11 says that her husband fully trusts her. Her reverence for the Lord and spirit of godliness has set a tone that makes her husband comfortable with her enough to bear his heart and soul.

Out of the twenty-two verses in the virtuous woman's profile, the only verse that addresses her conversation is verse 26: "She speaks with wisdom and faithful instruction is on her tongue." That verse alone says a lot about the Virtuous Woman. One of the characteristics of my friend, Renee, and other women like her, is that they are deliberate in speech. Because of their reverence for the Lord, they are careful to say only what God instructs them to and refrain from what they have not been led to say. They exercise remarkable self-restraint. There is no perfect woman, but overall, they walk and talk in step with the Holy Spirit.

"She watches over (looks after, spies out) the affairs of her household and does not eat the bread of idleness" (verse 27). This woman is actively involved in the personal lives of her family. The word watch is like that of a guard. Nothing can enter her gate that violates the Word of God and harm those she protects. The Christian woman's home is a haven of rest and a place of safety. Perhaps that is why Sarah told Abraham that Hagar and Ishmael should leave. "But Sarah saw that the son whom Hagar the Egyptian had borne to Abraham was mocking, and she said to Abraham, 'Get rid of that slave woman and her son, for that slave woman's son will never share in the inheritance with my son Isaac'" (Genesis 21:9–10).

The Virtuous Woman looked after her family. She cared for her husband, children and servants. Her husband lacked nothing of value. She planned ahead to ensure that her family was properly clothed for the winter and their future. She traveled far, if necessary, to get the best quality of food for her family. Then rose early to provide food for both her family and servants. She extended that same love outside her home by giving to the poor.

The virtuous woman is an asset to her family. In business, an asset is defined as a resource that directly or indirectly generates additional revenue. She brings to life Genesis 2:18, when the LORD God said, "It is not good for the man to be alone, I will make a helper suitable for him." We see this principle clearly in Jethro's counsel to Moses, "But select capable men from all the people—men who fear God, trustworthy men who hate dishonest gain—and appoint them as officials over thousands, hundreds, fifties and tens. Have them serve as judges for the people at all times, but have them bring every difficult case to you; the simple cases they can decide themselves. That will make your load lighter, because they will share it with you" (Exodus 18:21–22). The virtuous woman used her natural abilities for income, purchasing property and gardening. Her husband was able to entrust her not only with his heart but also his property and the care of his family and home.

In 1 Peter 3:3–4, Peter exhorts wives to embrace and exercise the inner beauty of a gentle and quiet spirit. First Thessalonians 4:11 says to make it our goal to lead a quiet life. The Christian woman who honors and trusts the Lord is calm and at peace with God. "But the wisdom that comes from heaven is first of all pure then peace-loving, considerate, submissive, full of mercy and good fruit, impartial, and sincere. Peace makers who sow in peace raise a harvest of righteousness" (James 3:17–18). Being at peace with God renders her at peace with herself and the world. Her mind is not troubled, but at peace. Her heart is not agitated, but at rest. She finds strength in the Lord. In Matthew 11:29, Jesus says of Himself, "for I am gentle and humble in heart and you will find rest for your souls." That does not mean there is no trouble in her life, but rather, in the midst of the trouble, she can have peace. As a woman at peace with God, she will not only be at peace with the world and herself, but she will also be a conduit of peace.

In Matthew 6:1, Jesus says, "Be careful not to do your acts of righteousness before men, to be seen by them. If you do you will have no reward from your Father in heaven. Do not let your left hand know what your right hand is doing" (Matthew 6:3). A Christian woman knows how to quietly move in and out of her roles without drawing attention to herself because her goal is to please God while serving others. When she serves dinner, her family does not experience the painstaking details of her labor. When she is offended, she gracefully smoothes over it. She allows others to experience the power of forgiveness without being asked. She generates the power of love through a quiet life. Quiet does not mean timid, but rather settled. She is not easily rattled, but secure in God's love. She understands her purpose and keeps to the path. She's meek, yet strong, quiet, but honest. We model Christian virtue when we keep our emotions, speech and our behavior under control with a watchful eye (Philippians 3:13, 4:13).

The virtuous woman holds various roles and therefore has multiple responsibilities. As a woman, Christian, wife, mother, daughter, sister, and friend, each role brings with it various responsibilities and tasks. When God places us in these roles, we become accountable for each. We can look to Him to give us the wisdom and power to carry out each with precision and excellence.

You may be easygoing. You may not like to work hard. Perhaps you think the Virtuous Woman was a little too busy for her own good. Perhaps you find yourself everywhere, doing a little here and a little there, but with no sense of purpose. The Virtuous Woman was a woman of purpose. She possessed an internal purpose that quietly shaped the quality of her life and the hearts and lives she touched. She knew where she was headed and why. In 1 Thessalonians 4:11 Paul instructs the Thessalonians to mind their business. As Christian women we must accept full responsibility for our lives and faithfully attend to the affairs of OUR life and OUR home.

At the end of 1 Thessalonians 4:11, we are told to work with our hands. This verse can be summed up in one word—"diligence." To manage a home is work. It requires spiritual, mental, emotional and physical effort. Late nights and early mornings are no strangers for the Christian woman. Proverbs 21:5 states, "The plans of the diligent lead to profit." When we accept the challenge, the Scripture says, we win respect of outsiders and are not dependent on anyone. As Christian women, we cannot depend on someone else to do what God has placed in our charge. The Virtuous Woman reverenced the Lord, and diligently looked after her family and her home. The results?

Her children arise and call her blessed; her husband also, and he praises her. "Many women do noble things, but you surpass them all." Charm is deceptive, and beauty is fleeting; but a woman who fears the LORD is to be praised. Give her the reward she has earned, and let her works bring her praise at the city gate (Proverbs 31:27–31).

PRAYER

Dear Lord, You have designated me as the home manager of my family. Scripture says that a wise woman builds her house, but the foolish woman tears it down with her hands. Please help me cater to my home and family in a manner that is pleasing to you. Help me faithfully and unconditionally love the people in my home and to use the knowledge, abilities, and gifts that You have given me. Grant me vision to see the greater picture, insight into the people in my home, perseverance when times get hard, and endurance for the duration of my call. I give You the glory for the great outcome.

SCENARIO, "MARRIAGE RETREAT?"

Following worship service a young lady approaches you and shares that she has observed your family from afar and admires the love and joy you emanate. She further shares that the reason she is coming to you at this time is that a young man she has been dating for a little over one year has asked her hand in marriage. She says she loves him very much, but is afraid. She says she grew up in an unsaved household with a lot of contention and that she isn't sure she knows how to be a good wife and mother. But she knows that she does not want to end up with the kind of family she grew up in. What encouragement could you give this young bride-to-be?

CHAPTER 6

Taking Personal Responsibility for Your Life

*L*ife is a gift from God. Breath, time, a sound mind, emotion, and a free will are just a few aspects of what we know and define as life. When we accept and affirm that life is indeed a gift from God, we affix to it a healthy measure of respect and take personal responsibility for it.

LIFE IS A GIFT FROM GOD

- Man was created by God (Genesis 1:27; 2:7).
- Man was created in the image of God (Genesis 1:27).
- Man was blessed by God (Genesis 1:28).
  With the exception of Adam and Eve, every man came by means of childbirth. Scriptures say that

children are a blessing from the Lord. The fruit of the womb is his reward (Psalm 127:3).

- Man was redeemed by God. Jesus Christ died and was raised from the dead to give man new (eternal) life (John 3:16; Ephesians 2:8).

When the Christian woman takes personal responsibility for her life, she accepts that she is accountable to God. Each of us will stand before God one day and give an account for our life (Ephesians 5:15; Luke 16:2; Romans 14:11–12; Hebrews 4:13; 9:27–28; Revelation 22:12). While there is no condemnation for those who are in Christ, we will give an account for our life and receive rewards based on the quality of our service (Romans 8:1; 1 Corinthians 3:12–13). The following are ways we are accountable to God:

- Our time (Genesis 6:3; Psalm 139:16; Ephesians 5:16),
- Our attitude (1 Samuel 16:7),
- Our choices and decisions (Ephesians 5:17; Romans 12:2; Philippians 2:12),
- Our resources (Romans 12:6a; Proverbs 3:9–10; Luke 16:2),
- Our body (1 Corinthians 6:19–20; Romans 12:1; 1 Corinthians 3:17), and
- Our words (Matthew 12:36–37).

When a Christian woman chooses not to take personal responsibility for her life, she exists with a lack of regard for her obligations to God, her family and for herself; she does not take the quality of her choices seriously. A Christian woman who does not take personal responsibility for her life is irresponsible. She chooses to allow her emotions, circumstances, people, the world, even Satan to govern her. Our emotions, circumstances, other people, the world and Satan can influence any of us, but to be controlled by any of them is unwise. The Christian woman who does so, forfeits her God-given ability to think and make choices. She gives the influences of her life license to exercise authority over her until she is no longer the executor, but rather the victim. Consequently, those influences shape her attitude, behavior and choices, rather than God. It is at this juncture that we lose many of our battles as Christian women.

While participating in a group discussion on depression at a Bible conference, a woman began to describe a woman she knew who had not only succumbed to the circumstances of her life but felt powerless in them. Listening to the case, it became clear that this woman had been caught and had fallen victim to her circumstances as well as demonic influences. If she had believed, embraced, and walked in the knowledge of who she was in Christ, who God is and His commitment to her, perhaps she would have had the faith and courage to stand mentally, and emotionally despite her circumstances. She then would have been able to make the necessary decisions regarding them. I say perhaps because there are certainly other contributing factors to consider when addressing persons suffering from depression.

Christian women must be strong in the Lord, not loudly religious, but knowledgeable and steadfast in the faith. If we are going to be useful for the Lord, we must be sure and steadfast concerning God's Word. We can neither vacillate nor compromise our faith and commitment to Christ. Only then will we have the stamina to weigh our emotions, be selective in our circumstances, resist antichrist movements and philosophies for the modern day woman, and recognize and refute Satan's ploys. No one can do it for us. It's a solemn internal and personal resolve each of us must individually make. It is the anchor to taking personal responsibility for our lives. It will determine the quality of our lives (our attitudes, behaviors, and choices) for the duration of our lives.

TIME

The Christian woman has to be mindful of time and how she spends it. Recently, I was reading a book on the life of Benjamin Elijah Mays, mentor of Reverend Dr. Martin Luther King Jr. The book covered the life of Dr. Mays and his contributions to higher learning on behalf of the African-American community. As I looked at the photos and read his life accomplishments, I quickly realized how little time we truly have on earth (Psalm 90:10). What at some point seemed like a long span of time to me, suddenly diminished to a mere fraction. At that moment I gained even a greater respect for my life with regard to how I utilize my time.

Each day is a gift from God. It is a new dawning. Imagine your hands cupped as though you were going to scoop water from a stream. But instead of water, God reached down from heaven to pour into your hands time like grains of sand until your hands were full. You have two choices, to hold onto it to try and keep it from slipping through your hands or to make good use of it before it is gone.

Time is a precious commodity (Ephesians 5:16). Everyday we live, God has chosen to pour out to us a fresh measure of time. Don't waste it by holding onto things like anger, resentment and worry, while time is simultaneously slipping away. Women have to be particularly careful because we are emotional beings. Practice leaving the problems of yesterday behind. This does not necessarily mean that our circumstances have changed, gone away, or that we should ignore and not do what is right regarding them. We must give God our cares so that our hearts and minds are free to experience God's wonders. "I wonder what new things God will teach me today? What will I see that until now I never understood?"

Order and structure how you use your time. Tomorrow is not promised (James 4:13–15). Be sure to do those things that are important to God. Be diligent, do not procrastinate and avoid being negligent. Wear a watch, set times to complete a task and be sure to stick to it.

Equally important, be careful not to live in the past, but rather use it as a stepping stone of lessons learned for the present and the future. Do not pass up the opportunity to live today. Learn to live the moment, not just for the future. Listen to the voices of children playing or the morning melody of the birds. Smell the air, feel the breeze as it brushes against your face. Take the time to give a glance of love, a pat of encouragement, or a tender smile.

Everyday when we open our eyes, we can rejoice over God ushering us into a new day to experience new lessons. When we close them at night, we can be thankful for what our eyes have seen, our mind has learned and what our heart has felt and understood, despite personal circumstances and sometimes due to them. Let your daily prayer be, "Lord, let how I know You now, and how I'll know You then be no big change." Set as a goal to live life in such a way that you don't fear death, but rather welcome it as you would a special guest at your front door.

ATTITUDE

While perusing the newspaper one day, it dawned on me just how important a healthy attitude influences our lives (Philippians 4:8). Within that day's news, there were life circumstances that warranted the individuals involved to make choices that would impact their life. A 78-year-old woman who had earned a doctorate degree, administered a scholarship, and taught kindergarten through college, was now going to attend her 8th college. A 38-year-old male police officer committed suicide on the spot after losing fifteen to twenty thousand dollars at a casino. Finally, a 35-year-old orthopedic surgeon's car was flattened under a rig. He escaped fatality by ducking and lying down during the collision. Officials were amazed at his ability to maintain his presence of mind. What was distinguishing about each was each individual's attitude concerning themselves, their life and their circumstances.

The Christian woman taking responsibility for her attitude recognizes that there is something she must do. In this life, you must possess a strong will to live and enjoy life regardless of the nature of your circumstances. No person can give that to you. That kind of attitude is available to us from God, but we have to submit to and appropriate it.

Recently, my dad and I had to take care of some family business for him in four major areas of his life: his occupation, housing, a medical situation from when he was in the Navy, and burial arrangements for the time of his death. As we spoke to each adviser, we received difficult truth from each. We were both taken aback. However, I could not reveal my dismay. As I drove him home, the Holy Spirit quietly reminded me, "But God." Then I remembered. In all the information we received, the missing variable was God. His promises came back to me, "Now unto Him who is able to do exceeding and abundantly above all we can ask or think" (Ephesians 3:20); then, "eyes have not seen, ears have not heard neither has entered into the hearts of men what God has prepared for those who love Him" (1 Corinthians 2:9); and "I was young, but now I am old and I have never seen the righteous forsaken nor his seed begging for bread" (Psalm 37:25). I resigned myself to be happy, to rest in His presence, and to be content with God's management of my dad's and my life.

Taking responsibility for our attitude is a choice each of us can make. When faced with difficult circumstances the normal response is to cry, fret, or worry. But we can't stay there. Once we have given it and ourselves to God and sought His face (often times more than once), He responds. We can make the decision to believe God by faith or to continue to look at our circumstances. If the latter, our circumstances begin to dominate our thinking and in essence, control us. Once again, we become victims. We cannot afford to allow the negative attitudes or offenses of others determine our attitude or behavior. Nor can we allow them to take away our freedom to act in a manner pleasing to God. Remain sober and be alert.

Feed and foster a positive attitude (Philippians 4:8). Circumstances will not always be to our liking. People will not and cannot meet our every need. There will be days when we feel alone or like we woke up on the wrong side of the bed. Finances, sickness, our menstrual cycle, the weather, or what we ate the night before all have the potential to cast a cloud over our day. Be determined to make everyday count. Start it off with the Lord. Take everything to Him. He will show you when life deals you peanuts, how to make peanut butter or if lemons, how to make lemonade. Daily repeat and believe, "This is the day the Lord has made, let us rejoice and be glad in it" (Psalm 118:24).

Be thankful to the Lord in your circumstances. The Scripture says that this is His divine or permissive will concerning you (1 Thessalonians 5:18). If we believe God is good, that He is always in control of all things at all times, the Scriptures teach that nothing can separate us from His love. We can be thankful knowing that our all-knowing, all-sufficient and loving heavenly Father knows and will do what is best toward us. When we have the desire to be thankful in our circumstances, we see the will of God clearer and put our hearts at ease.

My eldest son has a tremendous outlook on life. As a toddler, he had fun just being by himself. When there appeared to be nothing or no one to entertain him, he created fun. When reprimanded, he would come to his dad and me and say, "What are we going to do now?" Not all of us were born with such a resilient personality; however, if we are going to make our life count, we must exercise that kind of determination and be willing to laugh at ourselves.

CHOICES AND MAKING DECISIONS

Life comes with a multitude of choices and with the choices, comes the need to make decisions. When making decisions, we may find ourselves in one of two categories: either we make quick, rash and emotional decisions or we would rather not make any decisions at all. Either one can be harmful.

Recently, I saw a woman on a talk show who possessed a logical and methodical process for making decisions. But at the point of decision, she was afraid of making the wrong one. As a result, she made no decision—or so she thought.

Perhaps we do not like making decisions or we prefer for someone else to make decisions for us. Perhaps we are afraid or would rather not be bothered with the details involved in making a decision. Or perhaps we prefer a quiet, make no waves approach to life. Realize that in making no decision, we have in fact, made our decision.

Ignoring and putting off decisions or making quick, rash and emotional decisions won't make life better but will only complicate matters in the long run. We can take hold of the responsibility to make choices and decisions that give meaning and life.

God has given each of us a mind to think, a free will to make decisions, and the Bible for wisdom, direction, and life application (2 Timothy 3:16). Before making a decision, pray for God's wisdom, will and direction, (Philippians 4:6). Count the cost by gathering all the information possible before making a choice. Calculate the outcome as if the choice were affirmed. Then ask yourself, "What would be the consequences if I were to reject the option?" If others are involved, exercise consideration and respect. When you have reached what you believe is the answer or solution, take it to God. Let Him know what you have come to, then wait for

His response. This is a good time to seek wise counsel, but only after the previous steps are completed. The aforementioned steps will keep you accountable for thinking for yourself. They will hold you responsible for making decisions and trusting God rather than man. Once you have received the counsel, go back and lay everything before God. You will know what to do, because the Spirit of God will be at work and if it is God's will, what you gain from your research, the counsel you receive and what you receive from God will line up on one accord. Then follow through and make a decision with the knowledge you have obtained.

Exercising our freedom to think and make choices does not, however, give us license to be self-willed such as in the pro-choice movement on abortion. The act of abortion is not a freedom of choice alone, but an act of violence that should be addressed as any other first-degree murder offense. When a citizen chooses to use his or her rights to harm the life of another heart-beating and braining-functioning individual, they have abused their freedom of choice.

In the court of law, any individual committing an act of violence against another is subject to prison or death. Biblically, for the person using his or her rights to take the life of another (with the exception of war), his life was required of him (Leviticus 24:17).

Life support systems are used for comatose patients all of the time. The only time that life support is removed is when the patient has been declared brain dead, when the patient has a living will that gives consent to do so under such circumstances, or when a close relative chooses to do so under those same circumstances. Pregnant women are the life support system for their babies until the time of their birth. That by no means makes the infant less of a person with rights and privileges for life. The infant has a functioning brain and beating heart (Psalm 139; Jeremiah 1:5). Studies show communication with the infant while in the womb affect the infant. It is assumed that as the voice for our unborn fetus, we will make choices for his or her welfare just as there are living wills and executors to speak on behalf of a comatose patient.

The law of God sets a standard of holiness and righteousness. By it, the Christian woman can recognize good from evil. Therefore, when making choices, she can know what is right, or at least where to go to discover what is right. Be willing to live with the outcome of your choices. If you are committed to doing God's will, trust in His grace when you make a mistake. When you sin, ask for mercy, but be willing to accept His discipline.

Be self-controlled. Choose what your attitude, behavior and choices should be and stick with them. Do not vacillate. Always be willing to listen to sound advice. As a Christian, each should line up with what the Bible teaches regarding your circumstances. Remember that there is no human being, Christian or non, walking this earth who has not made mistakes. No mistake or sin is unredeemable or unforgivable by God. Do not allow the fear of failure keep you from making decisions. The Bible says, though a righteous man fall seven times he gets back up (Proverbs 24:16). So the next time you move to make a quick, rash and emotional decision, STOP! SLOW DOWN. This will be hard at first, but necessary. When you are tempted to put off making a decision, call yourself to action. You may have to begin slowly until you gain consistency and build confidence.

PRAYER

Dear Lord, please forgive me for not taking responsibility for my life more seriously. I have been frivolous with my body, time, talents, resources, and words. I have allowed my emotions, my circumstances and other outside influences to determine my attitude, behavior and my choices. You have made it clear that I am responsible for me. One day I will see You and I want to hear You say, "Well done." But, I need Your help. Help me to stand up and take hold of the reins of my responsibilities as I rely on You for wisdom and strength. I love You, Lord. I want to fulfill the number and quality of my days according to Your will. Thank You for giving me life. Thank You for the double blessing of eternal life. Thank You for a second chance.

SCENARIO, "HELPING SISTER"

Your neighbor, Cathy, is a model wife and mother. You have observed her and her husband praying together by the car on occasion. Before leaving home for work (a part-time job in nursing that affords her to use her gift for caring for people while managing her home and family), Cathy walks the children to their bus stop. You take note of her affection toward them and their love for her. One morning you notice while walking back from the bus stop, she is crying. You go out to inquire about her distress at which time she shares with you her burden for her twin sister. "My sister says she is not ready to settle down and be a "church girl" like me. She says that she is still young and has things to do and that she wants to be free. Unfortunately, exercising her "freedom" has caused her to incur outrageous debt." They grew up together and as little girls did everything together. "She is family." Cathy expressed the obligation she felt to help her sister financially. But she knew that if she and her husband continued to help, it would drain their savings. Cathy's husband has expressed his frustration. Now Cathy feels torn between the two. What advice would you give to Cathy?

CHAPTER 7

Personal Management

*L*ife is a trust. Taking personal responsibility for it requires effective personal management. To manage is to handle or direct with a degree of skill, to exercise executive, administrative, or supervisory direction for the purpose of accomplishing one's goal.

The following scriptural passages give us direct insight into God's perspective on life and time management:

In Genesis 1:28, God blessed man and commanded him to multiply and rule over the earth. God gave man authority, instruction, and skill for managing life on earth.

In Luke 12:35–48, Jesus teaches through the parable of a master's pleasure in finding his servant ready, watching, and doing what he was entrusted with when his master returned. That servant was placed in charge of everything his master possessed, just as Joseph was placed over his master's possessions and later given the place and authority second only to the ruler of Egypt. On the other hand, the servant who knows his master's will and does not get ready or does not do what his master wants will be beaten with many blows.

In Mathew 25:14–30, Jesus teaches through another parable of a man entrusting his servants with his property. Both the servant with five talents and the one with the two talents made good use of their endowment. In turn, they were rewarded for their efforts. Meanwhile, the third servant who was given one talent buried his. What he had was taken away and he was thrown outside into darkness.

Likewise, in Luke 16:1–15, Jesus presents a parable of the rich man, whose manager was wasting his possessions. That manager was fired for managerial negligence. While this passage addresses Israel's leadership, we are wise to take the principle to heart.

Life and eternal life are gifts from God. From the passages shown, we can see that God is explicit in regard to us managing our responsibilities and resources, which ultimately belong to Him. "Now it is required that those who have been given a trust must prove faithful" (1 Corinthians 4:2). "A faithful man will be richly blessed" (Proverbs 28:20).

Managing ourselves involves arranging our lives with the order and tools that efficiently produce an effective product. Good management is skillful living. It requires a finely tuned instrument, namely, a healthy mind, a fit body, and obedience to the will of God. Below, three key principles are identified for securing good personal management.

Personal management at its best begins with acknowledging God and that He is sovereign (Romans 11:33–12:3; Job 35:7; Psalm 111:10; Proverbs 31:30; Ecclesiastes 3:14; Luke 12:4–5). Whether we received life through pro-creation or both pro-creation and salvation, we must acknowledge the authority of an omnipotent (all-powerful), omniscient (all-knowing), and omnipresent (everywhere at the same time) God and that He is the author of everything except sin. Affirming the following facts is essential for a blessed life: 1) God created the universe; 2) God made man; 3) God made provisions for a second birth (Salvation through His Son); and 4) we need Him.

Personal management at its best, includes a personal faith in Jesus Christ, God's Son, for salvation (Corinthians 3:11). Jesus Christ's death and resurrection is God's provision for reconciling man back to Him. To go through life without Christ, despite personal skill, life accomplishments, and moral character, is futile.

Personal management at its best, is taking personal responsibility for living in obedience to the Lord by faith, not by our feelings or by what we see (Matthew 7:13–29; 16:23–26). Personal management also encompasses carrying out our biblical responsibilities as a Christian single, spouse, mother, widow, or single-parent, and the utilization of our time, talents, spiritual gifts, and resources to serve the Lord within our family, church, community, and when necessary, for obtaining wholesome employment. Managing our spiritual, physical, mental, psychological, emotional, financial, and social well being all contribute to good personal management.

The following provides a good start for ensuring all aspects of good personal management.

Spiritual Management

Spend time with God daily through prayer and reading the Bible. You can begin by listing on paper or in a personal journal those things that weigh heavily on your mind, that zap your joy and your peace. After setting them before the Lord, believe and trust that He will address them during your time with Him, within the course of the day or week. Spend time worshiping and honoring God from your heart with whatever you are grateful for no matter how big or how small. Read Scripture. Ask God to reveal to you what He wants to say specifically to you from the passage(s) you read. Next, spend time meditating on what you have read. Roll it over in your mind, then your heart. Next you want to ask yourself questions regarding changes you may need to make to align yourself with what you have read. Surrender to God's way. Continue to work it through daily until you have developed a new lifestyle. Do not give up on yourself when you fail, but rather learn from it so that point does not cause you to stumble or fall again. Let God know you accept His will and ask for His help.

Spend time in prayer. Do not allow the appearance of the urgent to rush or distract you. Spend time talking to God earnestly and thoroughly. Choosing or carving out the time to maintain a devoted prayer life is essential. Daniel prayed morning, noon, and night. It is a matter of what is important to God and to us. Spending time with us is important to God. Spending time with God in prayer must be important to you and me. When something is important, we find a way, if it is the last thing we do. It may mean you have to make some changes. It may mean getting up half-an-hour earlier.

I have a friend who spoke to a friend of hers diligently every morning before she went to work without miss, but not with God. I challenged her to make a change. Her priorities were out of line and her life choices reflected it. She changed them and is growing in her relationship and trust in the Lord. God is doing more for her than any friend could ever do.

We may need to talk to our girlfriend a little less and utilize that time with God. Maybe we could utilize that half-an-hour we spend watching television right after putting the children to bed. Look at your time and choices and choose a time to spend with God. He is waiting. He draws near to those who draw near to Him.

Refrain from spending time with God out of duty, "because it is the thing to do." Have you ever spent time with someone who you knew did not want to be in your company? Or they were preoccupied with other things? While it might have been the right thing to do, it doesn't make for a good relationship. It can turn out good if the persons are willing and honest with each other. Come to God with an earnest heart. If your heart is not there, but you want it to be, tell Him so. Jesus will honor your honesty. You will truly like getting to know the Lord. He meets us right where we are when we are earnest.

Unite with a local Bible-believing and teaching fellowship. Attend regularly; support your local church monetarily and look for a place or way you can serve. Be open and prepared to share the plan of salvation as you go.

Physical Management

Physical exercise enhances mental, emotional, and spiritual discipline. Develop a plan for doing what is necessary to be healthy. This may include seeing a doctor, losing weight, exercising, eating the right foods, and getting the proper rest.

The sun goes down, the trees and grass sleep through the winter and animals have periods of hibernation. God rested on the seventh day. The key is to know yourself. Know when your body is telling you to shut down. Do not ignore the signals it will give, such as a constant headache, forgetting what happened yesterday, depression, a lack of motivation, or falling asleep at the stop light. No one will know better than you when you need to take a break. Don't try to be a martyr or look for others to notice how tired you are. We are responsible for ourselves. When you see the signs, you have already gone too far. Know yourself well enough to do something before the signs appear. Just like a car has to be taken in every three thousands miles for an oil change, good body maintenance requires scheduling and taking regular periods for rest. Our bodies are like a machine. When it is run down, it affects every other area of our lives. Take care of the physical you.

Mental Management

A Christian woman must keep her mind healthy by occupying it with what is true and good. Engage in pure conversation with others. Refrain from living reclusively particularly if you are an introvert. Learn to respond to life's curves intelligently rather than emotionally. It is important to discipline your mind to think things through. Ask yourself, "What effect will the decision I am about to make have on others, particularly those in my home?" Read, read, read. Reading keeps us informed and our minds alert. It broadens our knowledge base and enhances our vocabulary and conversation. Good mental management will promote healthy decision making.

Psychological Management

Feed your mind on what is true, right, good, admirable, and praiseworthy. Time for daily pampering, such as a quiet walk, painting your nails, watching a wholesome movie, reading a wholesome book or magazine article, writing a letter or sending a note, calling a

135

friend, going to the mall, meditating, napping, having tea, etc., is essential to your psychological well being.

Set aside time each year for a three-day to one-week getaway without your mate and the children. Take this time to be renewed in the Lord, to evaluate your life in light of your goals and responsibilities. Evaluate the progress of your goals regarding your family (husband and children). Then set new or re-establish old goals for you, your relationship with your husband, and your children's development. Take some time to get refreshed and reorganized in order to manage you, your family, and home for another year.

Emotional Management

Our emotions are a gift from God. Our emotional responses can be a reflection of what we think (internal) and of our environment (external). Living devoid of emotion makes us mechanical and hard, lacking the finesse to develop and communicate through human relationships.

Our emotions also influence our physical health and behavior. Do not allow various moods to dictate your behavior, but rather respond to them intelligently. Emotions fluctuate. Hormones, body chemistry, diet, hunger, sin, sleep loss, and trauma can all affect the wholesomeness of our emotions. Strive to manage your emotions intelligently and with Scripture.

Financial Management

Live and keep your family on a balanced budget. Do not strive for wealth. You may desire to improve your financial standing and can do so through wise money management that includes: tithing, saving, education, investing, and eliminating debt. Three areas that may not appear to be financial principles that, however, affect the believer's finances are obedience to Scripture, serving God, and giving.

Young couples should plan and be patient in growing wealth and goods. Be willing to sacrifice wants and desires when necessary. Too much money should not be spent on perishable items such as fast food, junk food, clothing, and new cars. There is no return on items like these. Plan to buy a home rather than renting one. There is no equitable return when renting your place of residence; however, if the monetary means for purchasing a home is not available, do not be discouraged. Be thankful and rejoice in the Lord for God's daily provisions for you and your family. (There are programs for purchasing a home with no down payment, particularly for first-time homebuyers.)

If you have young children, it is good if you can be at home with them. Statistics show that latchkey children are more prone to get into trouble and substance abuse due to a lack of supervision. If you have young children and must work outside the home, do not allow yourself to be plagued with guilt, be ashamed, or beat yourself down. God's grace will aid and guide you and protect your children. You can make plans to go from full-time to part-time in the future, if possible, and encourage your husband in his work. Single parents can pray and look into work that can be done from home. Be a strong but loving disciplinarian; seek help and support from Christian friends, when necessary.

If young children are present and your family can manage on your mate's income, do not sacrifice the children's physical, emotional, and psychological needs for material gain. "A faithful man will be richly blessed, but one eager to get rich will not go unpunished" (Proverbs 28:20).

Social Management

Keep Christian women around you who love the Lord, not based on their financial status or personality. Be careful not to compare your life with the lives of other women. Each woman's circumstances, talents, gifts and resources vary. Therefore, responsibilities vary from woman to woman. The key is to responsibly manage what God gives you and to encourage your sisters. "Each one should test his own actions. Then he can take pride in himself, without comparing himself to somebody else, for each one should carry his own load" (Galatians 6:4–5).

Be sure to make room in your heart and life for women whose personality differs from your own. Relationships with women of various temperament and personality types can enhance our development and perspective. Allow women into your life whose spiritual commitment is stronger than your own for spiritual accountability and growth. Engage with women who are less committed to Christ without compromising your faith. Be committed to bringing another woman along in the faith. Lastly, invest time for reaching out and engaging with women who are non-believers. We are the salt of the earth and the light of the world. God's goal for us is that we win the lost.

Overall Management

Often we look at the areas of our lives to determine what comes first. We conclude that the spiritual should come first. So we organize our lives in an itemized manner with God first, our mates second, our children third. Then everything else pretty much gets tacked on in an order of what we deem important. I would like to present to you another perspective that I believe is a biblical one and one that will help you see the whole you, manage the whole you and utilize every part of you to honor the Lord. It is called a balanced life.

God is our Creator. When He created us, He created us with a body, mind, will, and emotions. He instructed us to control the earth (Genesis 1:28). God designed marriage, the first human relationship (Genesis 2:22–25). God designed man and woman to have children, creating the parent-child dimension of human relationships called the family. Looking at what God did, which one is man not responsible for? In the Old Testament we were taught to love God with all of our heart, soul and strength (Deuteronomy 6:5) and in the New Testament to love God with all of our heart and our neighbor as ourselves (Matthew 22:37). We have been instructed to make disciples (followers of Christ) of men. As Christians, we are to be godly women, respectful wives, and loving mothers. We are to use the gifts that the Holy Spirit has given us to exercise the character of Christ. What part am I not responsible for? The truth is, we are responsible for it all. God has assigned to all of us a window of time for doing His will, the mind to do it intelligently, His Spirit to do it with godly motives and character, the will to make the right choices and the body to carry it out.

It is all important to God. The Bible says, "But seek first his Kingdom and his righteousness, and all these things will be given to you as well" (Matthew 6:33). God and His will are the priority. After we are saved, we are to seek the righteousness of God for every area of our lives. I am responsible to God as a Christian, a Christian woman, wife, mother, daughter, sister, and for any other area He has entrusted to me. Scripture reveals God's will for each. We are to manage our responsibilities biblically and with the strength and skill He provides.

The picture then becomes a circular one, with Christ at the center of each. As a Christian it is important to worship God, to spend personal time with Him, to learn and grow, and to give back to Him in service and through paying tithes and offerings. For therein lies the wisdom and strength to fulfill all our other responsibilities. The Scriptures instruct Christian women to respect their husband and to submit to his leadership (Ephesians 5:22–33). As a Christian mom, we are instructed to love our children and manage our home (Titus 2:3–5). Which one is most important to God? While worship and serving God in ministry is important to God, I am equally responsible to God for loving my husband and children, and managing my home. What good have I done if I spend time worshiping God and serving in ministry, but in my home I disrespect my husband, I mistreat my children and am a lazy home manager. Listen to what God says, "Therefore, if you are offering your gift at the altar and there remember that your brother has something against you, leave your gift there in front of the altar. First go and be reconciled to your brother; then come and offer your gift" (Matthew 5:23–24).

We are responsible to God for every area of our life (Romans 12:1–2). Not only so, but because of who He is in me, He becomes a principle part of everything I do. He is the reason I do what I do and for determining how. Every aspect of my life belongs to God and it is up to me to make sure that each area of my life lines up with God's revealed will. We have the opportunity to serve the Lord in every area and with every aspect of our lives. As you set out to live to please God in every area of your life, He in turn will use your life to bring glory to Himself.

But I tell you the truth: It is for your good that I am going away. Unless I go away, the Counselor will

not come to you; but if I go, I will send him to you.
When he comes, he will convict the world of guilt
in regard to sin and righteousness and judgment:
in regard to sin, because men do not believe in me;
in regard to righteousness, because I am going to
the Father, where you can see me no longer; and in
regard to judgment, because the prince of this world
now stands condemned (John 16:7–11).

Chapter ten will instruct you how to align every area of your life with God's will and how to achieve and maintain balance.

Learn your personal strengths and weaknesses. Use your strengths, not boastfully, but rather humbly and with God-confidence. In other words, you and I know that apart from God granting us the ability, the mind and the strength, it would not be possible. Therefore, render service out of a heart of gratitude and not pride. A possible pitfall when functioning in areas of natural strength is the danger of operating in the flesh rather than in the Spirit. We operate in the flesh when we are self-reliant, and propelled by our own energy and ideas without seeking insight and wisdom from God. When operating in the flesh, we rely upon our own ability to pull off a task when in essence, just as with personal areas of weakness, we still must depend on God. It is God who takes what we do well to a greater and supernatural level, ultimately yielding infinite results.

Strengthen personal areas of weakness. The adversary will target his assaults in areas we are weak. Also, be mindful that in areas of weakness, God is strong. Therefore, those areas of weakness cultivate within us a need for dependence upon God. Do not think of your areas of weakness as a handicap, but rather as an asset that produces supernatural results when they become God's possession. Finally, maintain a balance of work, rest and recreation (Colossians 3:23–24). God's Word is true, His way is easy and His burden, light.

Now all has been heard; here is the conclusion of the matter: Fear God and keep his commandments, for this is the whole duty of man (Ecclesiastes 12:13).

PRAYER

Dear Lord, I must admit, some things have gone undone. I have spent so much of my time not realizing all that I am accountable for living in obedience to You. Much of my time and effort are unaccounted for. Often over-whelmed, I have neglected myself and blamed my job and my family for it. There are responsibilities as a Christian single, wife, mother, single-parent, and widow. I am responsible for using my natural and spiritual gifts, and for managing myself physically, mentally, emotionally, psychologically, socially, and financially. Help me to set order to what you have entrusted to me. Help me to manage every area of my life so whether it is the rapture or death, You will find me ready, watching and working.

● SCENARIO, "JUST WHAT THE DOCTOR ORDERED"

You wake up somber one morning with a tear falling now and then. As you go throughout the day, you work hard to feel happy and exuberant. That evening, there is no change. You pray and do all you can to shake it. The following morning, to your dismay, the fog is still there. You determine to take the day off from your normal routine to sit before the Lord with an open Bible and hear from Him. Reading God's Word has always been a pleasantry for you and while that is the case even now, by noon you don't see where God has addressed your problem. You resign yourself to some lunch. While washing your dishes, you look out the window and the spring flowers in bloom compel you to take a quiet walk. Upon your return, you open your Bible once again with the hope of hearing something from God through His Word. You read and read, but nothing seems to satisfy. The doorbell rings. The children are home from school and you must resume your usual routine: homework with the children, dinner preparation, husband home from work, family dinner, devotion with the children, shower, then bed. Perplexed, yet with a glimmer of sunshine you kneel at the side of your bed for prayer. You thank the Lord for getting you through the day but inquire why He did not answer your prayer. Calmed at that moment with a presence like the tranquil wind of an ocean breeze, you reflect over the day. God speaks to your heart and informs you it was He who had you take the day off; how it was He who enjoyed your presence as you sat quietly before Him; how He nudged you on for nourishment, and accompanied you on your walk. Then you were reminded, "He makes me lie down in green pastures, he leads me beside quiet waters, he restores my soul" (Psalm 23:2–3). Thank You, Lord.

CHAPTER 8

Overthrowing Life's Hindrances and Sin

Therefore, since we are surrounded by such a great cloud of witnesses, let us throw off everything that hinders and the sin that so easily entangles, and let us run with perseverance the race marked out for us. Let us fix our eyes on Jesus, the author and perfecter of our faith, who for the joy set before him, endured the cross, scorning its shame, and sat down at the right hand of the throne of God (Hebrews 12:1–2).

There are two kinds of runners in the sport of track and field: the sprinter who runs short distances and stresses maximum speed, and the long distance runner who runs lengthy races and requires endurance.

The Christian's "journey of faith" can be, as Paul and the writer of Hebrews denotes, equated with the long distance runner. And just as there are obstacles that interfere with a long distance runner finishing a marathon, so there are obstacles in the life of a Christian's "journey of faith" race. In the case of the Christian, the obstacles can be classified as hindrances or sin.

ATTITUDES	BEHAVIOR OR LACK OF	OBJECTS
fear, worry, envy, jealousy, apathy, pride, anger, self-righteousness, self-pity, malice, doubt, self-centeredness, poor self-image, bitterness, resentment, unforgiveness, apathy, greed, revenge, judgment	laziness, procrastination, busyness, sleep, cursing, smoking, drug-addiction, drinking, self-will, gluttony, adultery, fornication, lust, lesbianism, arguing idolatry, stealing, slander, gossip, lying, retaliation, shopping, breaking the law of the land	television, cigarettes, telephone, alcohol, education, drugs, sex, money, food, materialism, ungodly relationships, movies, videos, music, dress, books, and magazines, false religious beliefs (a good-luck charm, yoga, new age), inappropriate role model, drug paraphernalia

POTENTIAL HINDRANCES AND SIN

The list above is a sample of areas that restrain spiritual growth and effectiveness. Some areas are more of a problem to some than others. Some are a natural part of our sin nature. Some are learned behavior patterns passed down through our family line from one generation to the next. They are the ditches that cause us to stumble, the chains that hold us in bondage, and the poison that infuses our lives and the lives of the people we touch. In order to run the race of faith, the Christian woman must guard her heart and keep careful watch that when they appear, they do not linger.

HINDRANCES

A hindrance is something that slows or makes progress difficult. It serves to hamper, hold back, delay, impede, or interfere. There are some hindrances that are not, nor can be specifically identified as sin, but they keep us from fulfilling God's will. Watching television is not sin providing we select entertainment that does not violate God's Word, His Spirit in us, or our conscience. However, if watching television keeps us from doing what God says, it becomes a stumbling block—a hindrance that ultimately leads to sin. Rather than reading our Bible for one-half hour or going for a walk for our health, we may justify our need to see a favorite show just one more time. Only now we may have added our favorite snack, avoided incoming calls, or delayed dinner.

When being fitted to fight with Goliath, David knew Saul's armor would not work for him. It was too large. He could have worn it anyway. After all it was the King's suit of armor. However, he would not have performed at his best, and worse, he may have lost the battle and Israel would have become enslaved to the Philistines (1 Samuel 17:38–40). The success of the battle wasn't incumbent upon five stones and a sling or the King's armor, but on the Lord and David's faith to believe God and His will for Israel. The King's armor would have been a great hindrance for David—a hindrance from effectively doing God's will.

Some hindrances to keeping the faith are sin. Before birth, God made known to Samson's parents His will for Samson. He gave explicit details how Samson was to be raised. As a young adult, Samson spurned his parents' training and admonition. He developed a love for ungodly women and violated his Nazarite vow. His sin cost him pain, humiliation and, unfortunately, his life. However, in his last finale, he triumphed in faith (Judges 13–16).

When helping others address issues in their lives, much of what we share is from God's Word and extends from our love for Him and an earnest love for people. We also take joy sharing our personal victories. However, another area of reference we can be passionate about when helping others is our failures. How many times have we been adamant with our children, particularly our teenagers or young adults, because we do not want them to make the same grave mistakes we have made? I believe Samson, identified in the Hall of Faith in Hebrews chapter 11 would tell many of us a few things not to do. So, in order to remain faithful to the Lord and our profession of faith, how do we deal with the hindrances and sins that attempt to bind us? Let's take a look at Scripture:

> *If your hand causes you to sin, cut it off. It is better for you to enter life maimed than with two hands to go into hell, where the fire never goes out. And if your foot causes you to sin, cut it off. It is better for you to enter life crippled than to have two feet and be thrown into hell. And if your eye causes you to sin, pluck it out. It is better for you to enter the kingdom of God with one eye than to have two eyes and be thrown into hell, where their worm does not die, and the fire is not quenched (Mark 9:43–48).*

We live near a wooded area and, therefore, may encounter a field mouse during the winter months. To prevent a field mouse from entering the house, it is imperative that the house is adequately sealed and traps strategically placed to ensure captivity. One day I was giving one of my children an object lesson on not playing around with sin. I showed him the small mousetrap with bait and explained that the purpose was to catch the mouse. I told him that just as we laid a trap to ensure the mouse's captivity, Satan lays traps to ensnare us. And just as we laced the trap with bait for luring the mouse, the enemy of our souls sprinkles his wiles as bait to lure us in and keep us coming back for more. I warned my son that just like mice are tempted by the bait and ultimately trapped, if he played with sin he, too, would get caught in it and suffer harm.

Indeed, a few days later, the mouse was caught. My son was able to see first hand the consequences of not eradicating sin quickly. Likewise, in order to run the race marked out for us and to finish our course, we must confront the hindrances and sin in our lives seriously, purposefully, radically, honestly, thoughtfully, thoroughly, and completely.

Seriously

Although he was warned, Eli allowed his sons, priests of Israel, to continue serving in the Temple in their sin against God (1 Samuel 2:27–36). Both Eli and his sons were put to death. God warned Cain to take responsibility for his actions or sin would rule over him (Genesis 4:6–7).

Cain remained prideful rather than heed to the counsel of God and in the end murdered his brother Abel. Areas of hindrance and sin that are allowed to fester and grow can only lead to destruction.

Purposefully

The goal is to eliminate the source of the problem, consequently releasing one from sin's reign and its effects. A well-disciplined athlete keeps her eye on the goal. Her objective is to win. At no time will she risk looking back or to the side to view her opponents. She knows that the moment she glances away from the goal, she will lose her momentum and impede her progress.

Radically

In Mark chapter 9, notice that Jesus did not say cut off the sin, but cut off the hand, cut off the foot, pluck out the eye. The act of sin is not an isolated problem. By getting rid of what causes or leads to sin, the sin is uprooted. For example, it is known that being over-weight due to excessive eating is the sin of gluttony or greed. But what causes one to overeat? Most of us overeat simply because we're American. As funny as this may seem, it is true for two reasons: 1) America, compared to other countries, is extremely prosperous; and 2) culturally, Americans consume more food and collect more possessions than people on any other continent. But on a more personal note, many of us eat for the wrong reasons. My mother used to say, "Eat to live. Don't live to eat."

We eat for comfort. Feeling happy, sad, lonely, mad, tired, or bored often can lead to excessive eating. It is during these instances that time is taken from engaging in productive work or service and food becomes the substitute.

We can retrain our minds to think differently. When we are lonely, we can put our efforts toward building a friendship. When we are angry, we can take the time to pray, then position ourselves to be a blessing to the next person we encounter. When we are sad, we can immediately take our disappointment to Jesus who will affirm and fill us with His joy so that we are equipped to bring comfort to someone other than ourselves. If we are bored, we do well to establish goals, activate other passions or acquire new interests. We can get busy by getting involved in the lives of others. When we do, we eliminate unproductive time and refocus our attention and efforts away from ourselves. When we go to the root, we eliminate the source of the problem and decrease its probability to return.

Honestly

In order to take a radical approach towards the hindrances and sins that entangle us, we must be willing to acknowledge the truth and submit to God's Word. "If we claim to be without sin, we deceive ourselves and the truth is not in us" (1 John 1:8). David prayed when confessing his sin to the LORD, "Surely you desire truth in the inner parts" (Psalm 51:6a). "LORD, who may dwell in your sanctuary? Who may live on your holy hill? . . . who speaks the truth from his heart" (Psalm 15:1–2c).

An immature and inadequate confession of sin occurs when remorse is felt and expressed because we're caught and not because we have confronted ourselves with the truth. Neither is repentance feeling bad over our sin, yet remaining uncommitted to making a change. The Prodigal Son's condition brought him to his senses (Luke 15:11–24). He quickly prepared and set out to go to his father to acknowledge the sin he had committed against him. It was at that time the relationship with his father (a representation of God the Father) was restored.

Thoughtfully

"Or suppose a king is about to go to war against another king. Will he not first sit down and consider whether he is able with ten thousand men to oppose the one coming against him with twenty thousand? If he is not able, he will send a delegation while the other is still a long way off and will ask for terms of peace" (Luke 14:31–32).

We hear Christians testify how God miraculously delivered them from a form of substance abuse or some other sin. For those whom God has blessed this way, it is the supernatural act of the mercy and grace of God. For others, deliverance is a walk of faith, discipline, and hard work. Once we acknowledge the hindrance or sin (if the hindrance or sin is a longstanding way of life) we must count the cost and institute a plan for overcoming our area of weakness. Obesity, anger, nor any other sin will go away by prayer alone. A Christian woman must take responsibility for her choices and behavior (See chapter six, "Taking Personal Responsibility for Your Life").

Gideon had to begin believing, trusting, and obeying God rather than his fear in order to experience what God had already said was true about him—that he was a mighty warrior. Israel had prayed, God answered and sent a man for their deliverance. But that man had a responsibility. The LORD turned to Gideon and said, "Go in the strength you have and save Israel out of Midian's hand. Am I not sending you?" (Judges 6:14). By the hand of the LORD Gideon rescued Israel from her enemy, the Midianites (Judges 8:28).

Thoroughly

"God saw all that he had made, and it was very good. And there was evening, and there was morning—the sixth day" (Genesis 1:31). Thoroughly demands that there be no stone left unturned. All objectives and qualifications are appropriately addressed and satisfied. At the point of Christ's death on the cross, every prophetic Scripture about His birth, life and death was fulfilled. No prophetic inscription was left unaccounted for.

As with the start of anything new, the outcome is relative to how well instructions are followed. Eliminating any part of the process will hinder progress. In direct disobedience to God, Israel chose not to eliminate her enemies while taking the Promised Land. As a result, Israel took on their practices, became ensnared and was carried away in captivity. Obedience is an absolute for thoroughly uprooting personal hindrances and sin.

However anxious we are to rid ourselves of sin or hindrances, we must be sure to allow the necessary time for complete transformation. Change is a process requiring the application of God's Word to our situation faithfully. God works from the inside out. Change begins by renewing our mind with what is right and true

(Romans 12:1–2). Change is made in the heart when what is right and true in the mind is personally accepted and exchanged for old beliefs and convictions. Transformation occurs when our new beliefs and convictions are faithfully exercised until they become a way of life.

Completely

"It is finished" (John 19:30). Ah! Accomplishment. There is no satisfaction that can compare to coming to the end of a day having accomplished all we set out to do. Imagine approaching the last milestone of a daily two mile run, coming to the end of a long-term project, turning in the test of the last class in order to graduate from college, or the satisfaction of all the children being tucked in bed, on time and without any glitches. Such is the sense of fulfillment experienced when we have dealt completely with the hindrances and sin in our lives.

How many projects do we start only to set them on the shelf due to sheer boredom, or a lack of motivation, commitment and discipline to complete the task? Nowadays, we are afraid to be taken too seriously. We make impulsive promises with good intentions, but lack the commitment necessary for carrying them out. It used to be said, "Your word is your bond," meaning we could be depended on.

Where would we be if Christ had exercised this kind of liberty, lack of commitment, disloyalty, and instability? We trust Christ and depend on Him because of His proven character. He will do just what He has promised. The success of completing any task lies in our level of commitment and dependence on Christ. Imagine Christ's anticipation when He knew He was going back to the Father; His steadfast commitment when one of the criminals asked to be remembered when Christ came into His kingdom; His determination with the foreknowledge of the graves opening following His death; and His joy upon hearing the first sinner's prayer following His resurrection and ascension.

Conflicts, trials and temptations can pose threats by killing our motivation, stifling our progress and silencing our belief. Friends can pray and encourage us, but we have to do what is necessary to overcome hindrances and sin. No one can do it for us. We must not succumb to self-doubt, but instead believe that we can do all things (what is required of us from the Lord) with the help of the Lord. Be mindful that working on a problem or sin area does not disqualify you from service to the Lord and His people, unless it is something that would cause someone else to fall.

Scripture says that in order to be Christ's disciples, we have to hate even our own lives. We must become acquainted with self-denial, willing to endure the length of a task, move forward in the face of opposition and have the determination to get back up when we fall. All of these difficult choices the Christian woman makes to complete the task translate into commitment. Paul wrote, "I have fought the good fight, I have finished the race, I have kept the faith" (2 Timothy 4:7).

I spent twenty years developing my two oldest children with resolve, passion and commitment. Through laborious prayer, God's grace, and mercy, they were submitting to the training of their father and me. Not realizing it, I began to relax and take the peace for granted. Then God began showing me that I had put away my parenting manual too soon and was not exercising the parenting skills I used with my sons for my daughter who is seven years younger than my youngest son. God helped me understand that my job was not finished.

At Calvary, Christ sipped the wine-vinegar and having fulfilled the will of God, uttered solemnly yet victoriously, "It is finished" (John 19:30). Because of Christ, regardless of the nature of the task, we are more than conquerors through Christ who loves us (Romans 8:37). You and I can say to the hindrances and sins that hold us in bondage, "It is finished."

RUNNING WITH PERSEVERANCE

In Hebrews 12:1, we are told to "run" with perseverance the race marked out for us. The Christian journey is no stroll through the park. The Christian woman must have a sense of urgency, sobriety, and endurance (patience). We do not know when Jesus will call us home, the time of the rapture, nor the difficulty or longevity of our race. When Christ returns, He wants to find us ready, watching and working (Matthew 24:42–44). Keep going even when the going is tough.

While running the race marked out for us, we have been told to take note of the Old Testament saints in the faith. While observing the lives of Old Testament saints is encouraging and strengthening, only Jesus ran the race with perfection. He is our role model. When we look at and to Him, we have hope, strength, and courage. He ran and completed the race marked out for Him while enduring opposition from sinful men.

My family and I worked all day one Saturday cutting hedges. Branches were placed in the designated disposable brown paper bags. I called to have the bags picked up. But because the amount we had was the minimum, I was told to place them with our regular trash pickup. The trash men came on a Monday and said they would not take the bags but that another department would pick them up on Friday. I explained that I was told to put them out with my regular trash. They told me they didn't know who I was talking about and that they would not take the bags now because of the brown paper bags. Anxious to get rid of the trash, I asked if I might change the bags so that when they came around across the street they could take the bags then. They changed their minds and said they would take the bags as they were, but I would have to pay if they were fined because the trash was in the wrong bags. I informed them that I would not pay the fine if they took them as they were because I offered to change the bags. They accused me of not listening or believing them. I explained I had simply shared what I was told on the telephone by the department but respected their voice and experience. I came in the house baffled. They accused me of doing wrong, and when I tried to right my wrong, they argued with me. When I tried to show kindness and respect, they refuted that as well. I prayed and asked God to help me understand. He showed me how Jesus endured opposition from sinful men (mankind). There was nothing I could say to satisfy those workers. They were bent on being difficult. I do think I could have looked a little more like Jesus had I simply chosen to be patient, have my family re-bag the branches and put them out the following week.

Christ did not allow His opposition to become a hindrance. Not only did He endure opposition from sinful men, but He also endured the cross, the extermination of His life, and the shedding of his blood. He endured opposition and death in order to run and complete His race. He is the author of our faith. He set the example. A Christian woman can become quite discouraged. She wears many hats and engages in various relationships. These relationships require innumerable responsibilities and genuinely active and sensitive responses of affirmation against what can often appear as a lack of gratitude and understanding of the cost by those who still hold her by the strictest and highest of Christian virtues. A Christian woman must be internally strong in the Lord, understand her purpose and stubbornly, but graciously maintain her faith.

Jesus is the perfecter of our faith. He will make choices for your life and mine so that we might share in His holiness and be like Him. Just as Christ endured opposition and the cross, we are told to endure hardship as discipline, to submit and say yes to God, and to give Him thanks for His will recognizing that our lives and the individual lives of our family belong to Him.

I was in a car accident a few months ago. My car was totaled and I had to begin my search for another vehicle that would match my monetary resources at the time. I believe we should ask the Lord for what we desire, but this time, I did not want to ask the Lord for what I wanted, but rather that the Lord give me what He wanted for me. I was not concerned with the make or model of the car as long as it was sturdy enough for the amount of travel we needed to do. I knew that God had my life in His hands and that He knew more about His plan for me than I did. My desire was simply to give Him the honor of giving me what He wanted for me and to surrender to His will. As I fought to keep my will out of it and place myself in a position to receive whatever He chose for me; it really did not matter to me whether He chose economy or luxury; I just wanted to be in His perfect will. He gave Adam and Eve the Garden of Eden and Israel the land of Canaan. Surely, I could trust Him to do what was best for me. He blessed me with a beautiful luxury car with all the accessories and in my favorite color. When we surrender to what God wills and allows in our lives and in the lives of our individual family members, we are ultimately blessed. Remember that God is in control. He loves us and knows what is best. He can be trusted.

Let us strengthen our feeble arms and weak knees. We need lifted arms and strong knees to seek the help of the Lord through prayer. We cannot quit. We must not complain. We can make it. "Do everything without complaining or arguing, so that you may become blameless and pure, children of God without fault in a crooked and depraved generation, in which you shine like stars in the universe" (Philippians 2:14–15).

Finally, we must make level paths for our feet. Always be willing to obey God's Word regarding your circumstances. "Your word is a lamp to my feet and a light for my path" (Psalm 119:105). Determine a biblical and practical course of action. Stick to it.

In Bible times there was a process called girdling that male athletes and servants used when faced with the need to run.[1] The slave folded a cloth by the right breadth, then holding it at one end, while the servant took the other and laid it upon his side; then he rolled himself around, as tightly as possible, until he arrived at the slave, who remained immovable. While running, the ends of the outer garment were tucked into the girdle. The athlete or servant was adequately prepared to run.

Like the girdling of the athlete or servant, God's Word is a necessary tool for breaking through hindrances and sin that hold us hostage. Ephesians 6:14 reads, "Stand firm then, with the belt of truth buckled around your waist." The NAS reads, "Having girded your loins with truth." The girding process was known to not only simplify running, but to give strength to the body when engaged in severe bodily labor or exercise. We get a glance of its implications reading Job 40:7 when the LORD told Job, "Brace yourself like a man." Again where Psalms 93:1 describes the LORD as robed in majesty and armed with strength. Girding ourselves daily with the Word of God to run the race marked out for us is as necessary as food and water to stay alive. Just as the servant of the athlete remained immovable at the opposite end, so Jesus is at the other end. He remains faithful and His Word abides forever. We can trust Him to help us overcome the hindrances and sin that weigh us down.

PRAYER

Dear Lord, please forgive me for allowing other things and sin to control my life and for not taking their presence seriously. I have lived with these weaknesses for so long. When I tried to overcome them, I failed. I believed the devil's lies. I gave up believing I could ever be an over-comer. Thank You for the race You ran and the victory You have won, for dying on the cross for my sins, for being pierced for my transgressions and for being wounded for my iniquities. I believe You rose from the dead and by that same power, I believe that I am an over-comer.

SCENARIO, "LEAVING HINDRANCE BEHIND"

Olivia is a forty-one-year-old Christian woman who wants to return to school to complete her educational goal of acquiring a college degree. When Olivia graduated from high school, she went on to college. After she completed her first year, she married a young man who had already obtained his college degree. Olivia said she married him, fully intending to complete her education. Olivia's husband's job required travel. Rather than complete school, Olivia traveled with her husband and took classes intermittently.

In their third year of marriage, the two made the decision to start a family with the conviction that Olivia would be a stay-at-home mom. Olivia spent the next nineteen years raising her children before the dream of completing her college degree resurfaced. With much encouragement from her husband and children, Olivia stepped out to pursue her goal. Olivia became a full-time student. The first year, though challenging, was a successful one. Encouraged, Olivia set out to attempt her junior year. Then it happened. Olivia's parents needed care. This was the year that her son was graduating from high school. Her husband's job required travel once again and he also was pursuing his Master's Degree. Olivia served a vital role in ministry at her church, but had to cut back to go to school the previous year. There were needs in her congregation that her gifts could address. Olivia also home-schooled her nine-year-old daughter. Three days into her new school year, Olivia was told she could no longer bring her daughter to class with her. With no other options for caring for her daughter, Olivia had to withdraw from school. How would you encourage Olivia?

CHAPTER 9

The Grace of Humility

My heart is not proud, O Lord, my eyes are not haughty; I do not concern myself with great matters or things too wonderful for me. But I have stilled and quieted my soul; like a weaned child with its mother, like a weaned child is my soul within me (Psalm 131:1–2). Like a baby who settles in for the night after a feeding of warm milk from its mother's breast, the author has found total satisfaction in the Lord. When a Christian woman learns to depend on and trust the Lord to meet all of her needs, her once agitated and defensive spirit is transformed to a spirit of humility.

In its Greek form, humility means lying low. Metaphorically, it means (1) of low degree, brought low (Luke 1:52); (2) men of low estate, things that are lowly and of low degree (Romans 12:16; James 1:9); and (3) downcast or somber (2 Corinthians 7:6). Contrary to the world of fashion and design, the true essence of beauty in a woman rests peacefully in her willingness to embrace the grace of humility.

JESUS PRESENTS A COMPLETE PORTRAIT OF HUMILITY

When considering humility, is it an individual's economic or spiritual condition, emotional state or Christian character that is in question? No matter which form of humility is in question, God favorably addresses His commitment to each: He listens to their cry (Psalm 10:17) and He (lifts) exalts (Philippians 2:5–11). Consider Isaiah 61:1–3:

> *The Spirit of the Sovereign LORD is on me, because the LORD has anointed me to preach good news to the poor. He has sent me to bind up the broken hearted, to proclaim freedom for the captives and release from darkness for the prisoners, to proclaim the year of the LORD'S favor and the day of vengeance of our God, to comfort all who mourn, and provide for those who grieve in Zion—to bestow on them a crown of beauty instead of ashes, the oil of gladness instead of mourning, and a garment of praise instead of a spirit of despair. They will be called the oaks of righteousness, a planting of the LORD for the display of his splendor.*

Unfortunately, being poor in this country may mean not having the opportunity for higher education nor adequate medical provisions. Schools in most of our

urban communities lack appropriate educational resources. To further show our lack of tolerance for the
poor and weak, convalescent facilities are on the rise.
Many families are choosing now more than ever to place
parents and other family members, even young adults,
in nursing facilities rather than their own homes where
the convalescing can experience the loving support of
family.

Not only is Jesus committed to the meek and lowly,
but He is also a model of all aspects of humility:

Humility (low degree, brought low)

- He set aside His glory by lowering Himself and
  becoming 100% man, while being 100% God
  (Philippians 2:7).
- He never used his divinity for his personal
  advantage.

Humility (economic standing)

- He was born in a cave, laid in an animal feeding
  trough and wrapped in cloth (Luke 2:7).
- He was a carpenter and the son of a carpenter
  (Mark 6:1–3; Matthew 13:55–57).

Humility (spirit)

- He suffered hostility and rejection from his
  people and the world (Isaiah 53; Hebrews 12:3;
  1Peter 2:23–24).

Humility (character)

- Christ regarded our standing more important than His own (Philippians 2:3–6).
- Jesus Himself said that He came not to be served, but to serve and give His life a ransom for many (Mark 10:45).
- He was obedient to God, the Father, to the point of death on a cross (Philippians 2:8; Deuteronomy 21:23; Galatians 3:13).

God was well pleased with Jesus' humility (Luke 3:22) and highly exalted Him (Philippians 2:9–11; John 17:1, 5). Jesus' ultimate act of humility brings abundant and eternal life to those who accept the gift of salvation. This ultimate, triumphant, and exalted act of the grace of God resulted in the redemption of man. Mankind became an enemy of God at the fall. We were marred by sin, destined for death, and bound for hell until Christ died on the cross for our sins. This was the worst form of lowliness. Through Jesus' death and resurrection, He conquered death, hell, and the grave and made provisions for man's salvation. When we receive the gift of God, which is salvation through his Son, Jesus Christ, we become a child of God and are seated in heavenly places (Psalm 103:4; John 1:12; Ephesians 2:6–7).

MORE BIBLICAL EXAMPLES

Generally speaking, few of us aspire to the role of humility. What profit is there in being small or last, we muse. The world is unaccustomed to lifting and exalting others unless there is something to be personally gained, which, in essence, is not humility. The secular world dictates that we should interpret life by how it affects us or makes us look rather than how our lives affect others and reflect God's glory. Humility on the other hand dictates that we cast self down for the sake of lifting others, that we honor one another. When we cast self down to do the will of God and to elevate our brother, mankind sees the heart of Christ, which is God's agape love. Christ said, "But I, when I am lifted up from the earth, will draw all men to myself" (John 12:32). At that time, Jesus was referring to His crucifixion and resurrection; however, symbolically, we keep Christ before the eyes of man when we exercise humility toward God and one another. Consequently, mankind is drawn to Christ by His love and our love for one another.

In addition to Christ's example, the Bible contains other examples of individuals who exercised humility:

1) Mary, Jesus' mother: low economic standing and humble character—she found favor with God and was chosen to be Jesus' mother (Luke 1:46–55).

2) The Samaritan woman: considered by the Jews to be racially inferior and spiritually lost—Jesus saved her (John 4:4–26).

3) The woman caught in adultery: gender insignificant and caught committing adultery—Jesus did not condemn her, but told her to go and sin no more (John 8:1–11).
4) Rich young ruler and Lazarus: Lazarus was a beggar—Lazarus went to heaven when he died and rested in the bosom of Abraham (Luke 16:19–31).
5) Parable of the Pharisee and tax collector: Tax collector humble in character—He was justified (declared righteous) before God (Luke 17:9–14).

ESSENCE OF HUMILITY

The essence of humility is understanding who we are in light of God and what He has done for us. Joseph said when he was requested to interpret the Pharaoh's dream, "I can not do it . . . but God will . . ." (Genesis 41:16). David sat before the Lord after Nathan had reported the revelation of God to him regarding his inheritance from God, and replied, "Who am I, O Sovereign LORD and what is my family . . ." (1 Chronicles 17:16). When Isaiah saw the Lord, he said, "Woe to me! I am ruined! For I am a man of unclean lips . . ." (Isaiah 6:5). Elizabeth exclaimed when she beheld her cousin Mary, the mother of Jesus, "But why am I so favored, that the mother of my Lord should come to me" (Luke 1:43)?

Maintaining humility (an attitude of lowliness or casting one's self down) for us as Christian women rests in consistently reminding ourselves of who we are in light of God. It is recounting all God has done and made possible for us through the outpouring of His mercy and grace. Humility is a moment by moment commitment to submit and conform to the principles of God as outlined in Scripture.

The mind trained in humility toward God is focused. The mind trained in humility toward man is considerate and a good listener.

The heart trained in humility toward God is pliable and responsive. The heart trained in humility toward man is accepting, gentle, patient, caring, forgiving, and accommodating.

The will trained in humility toward God is subdued, disciplined and obedient. The will trained in humility toward man is obliging and giving.

Humility is abandoning self to meet the needs of others while placing our complete hope in the intervention of God on our personal behalf. This act of God is called grace and is extended to those who put their trust in Him. Humility is the willingness to make room, at any moment, in our life and heart for another. It is an attitude of love expressing itself through giving. A woman of humility is a woman rooted and grounded in the love of God.

"Dear friends, let us love one another, for love comes from God. Everyone who loves has been born of God and knows God. Whoever does not love does not know God, because God is love" (1 John 4:7–8).

HUMILITY IS A CHOICE

Humility towards God is a choice and precedes faith leading to salvation. We recognize our need for God when: (1) life is bigger than we are, (2) we need someone greater than us and our circumstances to bring peace and resolution to our lives and (3) nothing else fills the empty void in our soul. Through salvation, we receive eternal life (John 3:16–17), we become a child of God and receive power for Kingdom living (John 1:12; 14:16–17), we obtain a relationship with God, the Father and a home in Heaven (John 14:1–3, 6).

Humility is a choice and with the outpouring of God's love will generate a trusting heart that compels the Christian woman to surrender her will and perceived rights to the Lord peacefully. When I was a young teenager, my pastor preached a sermon about tithing. He demonstrated what God's ten percent looked like against my ninety percent. I walked away convinced that I wanted to give God what was due Him by faith. I received a ten-dollar allowance each week. That money was to be used for transportation back and forth to school. In my immature, albeit exuberant faith, I gave God my full allowance. I loved God and I reasoned that if He would bless me for just giving ten percent, how much more of the Lord's blessings I would experience if I gave Him everything I had.

Needless to say, when I told my mother, she did not share my enthusiasm, but rather reprimanded me for not using my head. However, she could not dissuade

174

my faith. I had the greatest feeling down inside of my heart and that was enough for me. By Thursday of the new week, my allowance was depleted. But I held on to what my pastor had taught . . . that God would meet my needs. My mom was in school at the time and had some studying that would prevent her from going to work that Thursday and Friday. Usually my sister and I rode the bus home. For the two days my mom was off, she came to pick my sister and me up from our bus stop. At fourteen, because of God's love, I learned to trust Him in the area of tithing and meeting my needs, two areas that have been the catalyst for exercising faith in other areas of my life.

Humility is a choice and precedes obedience to God. My husband had been out of work for several months. We were uncertain from month to month how we would meet all of our financial obligations, but God always provided. I had been a housewife for 15 years, but I wanted to encourage my husband by securing a job. I prayed for God to lead me. He did and I was hired immediately. Two months passed and the Lord let me know through several nudges that it was time to leave. I submitted by faith with the understanding that God had called me to write and to continue being a faithful wife and stay-at-home mom. After two months, the company presented me with an offer that was hard to refuse. At the time, my husband had not acquired full-time employment. I took a deep breath as God's will raced before me and declined the offer. God provided my husband with full-time employment within three weeks.

There are times when obeying the revealed will of God is met with opposition. The Christian woman must continue to recognize her need for daily and deliberate reliance on the Lord. To be obedient is to listen attentively and submit out of belief. Hebrews 5:8 says, "As a Son, Christ learned obedience through the things He suffered and is to all those who obey him the source of eternal salvation."

Humility is a choice and an after-effect of God's grace that will generate deeper commitment and greater faith. Abraham demonstrated great faith in his willingness to slay Isaac on the altar of Mount Moriah at God's request. Abraham's love for and faith in God had matured after witnessing God's unmerited favor throughout his life (Genesis 22:2; James 1:2–4). God called him out of Ur with promises of prosperity and honor (Genesis 12:1–3). God preserved the life of Sarah, his wife, as well as his marriage when he lied to the Pharaoh of Egypt by telling him that Sarah was his sister (Genesis 12:10–20; 20). God showed him favor when Lot, Abram's nephew, took what appeared to be the better land (Genesis 13). God delivered him from war against his enemies (Genesis 14:12–15:2), granted him the birth of Ishmael (Genesis 16:15–16; 17:18–20) and protected his nephew, Lot and family (Genesis 18:16–33). Abraham was granted the birth of Isaac (Genesis 21:1–5), in addition to the departure of Hagar and Ishmael (Genesis 21:10–20).

WHAT HUMILITY IS NOT

Humility is not to be mistaken for low self-esteem (Psalm 139:14). Moses was the meekest man to ever live. At the time of God's call, Moses possessed a lack of confidence despite God's desire to use him. In a like manner, Paul exhorted Timothy not to heed to his timidity, but rather fan into flame the gift of God that was in him (2 Timothy 1:5–7). First Peter 4:10 states, "Each one should use whatever gift he has received to serve others, faithfully administering God's grace in its various forms."

Tolerating brutal treatment is not humility. Jesus escaped when the Jews and the crowd wanted to attack him (John 8:59, 10:39, 12:36). Likewise, David fled from King Saul (1 Samuel 20:1) and his son, Absalom, who conspired to do him harm (2 Samuel 15:14). If you are treated in a way that is mentally, emotionally, or physically harmful, you should get help.

Giving and caring for the needs of others while neglecting our own need to be responsible for ourselves is not good personal management. God has given everyone resources for serving Him, taking care of personal needs and sharing with others. God will use us as a channel to bless other individuals. He expects us to help the impoverished and those who suffer misfortune. However, what service can the Christian woman give to God and her family if she does not take care of herself as well? Even, Jesus pulled away from the crowd at appointed times for prayer and solitude.

BROKENNESS

Humility can make its entrance into our life through brokenness and suffering, particularly when we refuse to voluntarily humble ourselves. "For whoever exalts himself will be humbled" (Matthew 23:12b; Luke 14:11; Luke 18:14; Hebrews 12:4–11). When we are broken, we recognize our sinfulness and sometimes the finiteness of our humanity.

Just as Saul did during his rule over Israel, when we choose to do things our way, we are acting independent of God. This expression of self-will is what the Bible calls pride.

Pride is humility's rival. It is lifting up self in mind, heart, or position. Pride manifests itself when we think more highly of ourselves than we ought and when we have little to no regard for the interest and welfare of others (Romans 11:17–21). When our heart is lifted in pride, we are in direct opposition with God, His character, and His will.

We do ourselves a disservice by being proud. God opposes the proud and will not endure anyone with a haughty look and an arrogant heart (James 4:6; 1 Peter 5:5; Psalm 101:5). God will remove those who rejoice in their pride and are haughty (Zephaniah 3:11). God will bring down the proud (Luke 1:52; 18:14; Psalm 18:27; Matthew 23:12). God will cut off flattering tongues and boastful lips (Psalm 12:3–4). God hates a proud look (Proverbs 6:16–17; 8:13). God is not close to the proud

(Psalm 138:6). God will destroy the house of the proud (Proverbs 15:25). God will punish the proud in heart (Proverbs 16:5).

A Few Examples

Naaman's refusal to wash in the Jordan (2 Kings 5:11–13).

Hezekiah displaying his resources (2 Kings 20:13; 2 Chronicles 32:31; Isaiah 39:2).

Haman's attempt to destroy God's people (Esther 3:5; 5:11,13; 6:6; 7:10).

King Uzziah burning incense on the altar of incense (2 Chronicles 26:16–21).

King of Tyre saying in his heart that he is a god (Ezekiel 28:1–10).

King Nebuchadnezzar's personal claim to the success of his kingdom (Daniel 4:30–37).

Brothers, think of what you were when you were called. Not many of you were wise by human standards; not many were influential; not many were of noble birth. But God chose the foolish things of the world to shame the wise; God chose the weak things of the world to shame the strong. He chose the lowly things of this world and the despised things-and the things that are not-to nullify the things that are, so that no one may boast before him. It is because of him that you are in Christ Jesus, who has become for us wisdom from God—that is,

our righteousness, holiness and redemption. Therefore, as it is written: "Let him who boasts boast in
the Lord" (1 Corinthians 1:26–31).

We can begin loosening pride's grip by aiming for
being devoted to the Lord in body and spirit, in what
we do and who we are. We have to voluntarily let go
of personal props we have allowed to define us. Define
us meaning they hold us up and make us feel secure
and valuable. They make us feel important and communicate that importance to our neighbor. They give
us a false sense of security and value and can vanish
instantly. Some of the props that we allow to define
us are, our personalities, possessions, goals, and
accomplishments.

There are many areas in our lives that we esteem. It
may be our body such as a nice figure, beauty, weight,
hair; our charisma; our possessions such as our car,
our house; our neighborhood; furniture; or the value or
beauty of the clothing or jewelry we own and wear. Perhaps it is our family: our parent's character or position,
our husband's or our position on the job, in ministry or
community affairs; our children's beauty, aptitude or
accomplishments or our intelligence, talents or spiritual gifts. As Christian women, we must determine not
to boast, to hide behind or be defined by anything or
anyone, but the Lord (1 Corinthians 7:34).

"Whoever humbles himself will be exalted" (Matthew 23:12b). God has beautifully illustrated the principle of humility even in nature. In autumn, the trees'

leaves turn yellow, red, purple, and brown and array the earth with their beauty. The color of the leaves stems from the root's knowledge that winter is on its way. The roots cease to take in nourishment from the ground causing the leaves to lose moisture, turn colors then disconnect from their branches to gracefully fall to the ground and replenish the earth.

During winter, when the temperature is below 32 degrees and moisture is in the air, snowflakes form. Each flake is uniquely designed echoing a melodious sound as they quietly and unassumingly dress the open air, each seizing their opportunity to descend and blanket the earth.

As in autumn and winter, spring ushers in its season for observing the principles of humility. Each raindrop obediently and gracefully casts itself down to water the earth.

What principles of humility can we learn from Scripture that are so beautifully illustrated in the life of Christ, even nature?

Each has a purpose,
Each is subject to God,
Each is willing to casts itself down,
Each empties itself in service,
Each is obedient to death (dying to self), and
Each is raised to new life

"And if the Spirit of him who raised Jesus from the dead is living in you, he who raised Christ from the dead will also give life to your mortal bodies through his Spirit, who lives in you" (Romans 8:11).

GRACE FOR THE HUMBLE

Following one of my classes, a student who was experiencing problems in her marriage came to me and shared that she knew God was calling her to humble herself and to become obedient to Him in her marriage. She expressed fear because, unfortunately, she had experienced several blows of disappointment at the hand of her husband. She had forgiven him, but was afraid she would be abandoned to do all of the giving.

As I listened, the Lord brought back to my mind how my husband and I have both suffered hurt at the hands of one another's foolish mistakes. I recalled once coming to what I thought was the end. As I peered into the recesses of my heart, I stumbled over the stones of a broken heart that did not have the ability to pull itself up by its bootstraps. My mind rested on Lazarus lying in a tomb and being dead four days, when Jesus, the resurrection and life, raised him from the dead. I went to my bedroom window and lifting my eyes to heaven prayed, "Lord, if you raised Lazarus from the dead surely You can give my heart new life. God immediately answered my prayer. He replaced my broken spirit and marriage with hope, life, and love as I trusted and submitted to His revealed will for me as a Christian wife.

"Humble yourselves, therefore, under God's mighty hand, that he may lift you up in due time" (1 Peter 5:6).

Often times we can think that our marriage and life are over when confronted with adversity. As a Christian woman living for the Lord, remember that absolutely nothing can come your way without God's permission (Job 1:6–12). Adversity of any kind is permitted and designed to strengthen and develop us. We learn something new about God and ourselves and are afforded the opportunity to become like Jesus (1 Peter 5:11; Romans 8:29). Do not resist, but determine to learn each principle God wants to teach you.

Adversity through a mate is sometimes the devil's tool to divide and conquer your family. His goal is to turn us against our mate by parading his weaknesses and faults before us. He will try to convince us to blame and lash out at our husband, when our real enemy is Satan.

Do not believe as a Christians that you will not suffer. That is a trap from the enemy to get us to doubt the faithfulness of God. If you are a Christian, but not in daily fellowship with the Lord, your adversity may be to bring you to repentance and help you grow. Adversity for the believer is never God's judgment or condemnation. His chastisement is an act of His love (Hebrews 12:5–6). If you are a non-believer, your adversity is used to help you recognize your need for Christ. When the Christian woman humbles herself and obeys the revealed will of God, she is able to say to Satan, just as Joseph said to his brothers, "You meant it for evil, but God meant it for good" (Genesis 37:5–8,23,28; 45:7–8, 50:20).

At the heart of humility is a deep and abiding trust in the love and sovereignty of God. For the Christian woman, it is a conscious commitment to render herself for the Master's use that He might display His splendor.

PRAYER

Oh Lord, forgive me for thinking myself to be something when apart from You, I am nothing. Forgive me for mistreating my Christian sisters, and for allowing anger, resentment, bitterness, quarrels, jealousy, envy, and pride to blanket my heart when I could not get what I wanted or thought I deserved. I have not considered Your will and heart nor have I stopped to consider the needs of others. I have not trusted You and Your sovereignty in my life. I have stood and defended my rights. I have made inroads for myself, rather than waiting on You. Lord, You are a perfect portrait of humility. Help me to become gentle and humble like You. Lord, I've often prayed to go higher, but I would like to change that prayer, Lord. Take me lower—for there are lilies in the valley of life. I know that Your grace will be sufficient for me, for Your power is made perfect in my weakness. I should rather boast in my weakness and Your glory. Lord, thank You for stopping by this place in my life.

SCENARIO, "DOWN AND OUT"

You leave your family on the slopes and retire to the lodge to warm your feet. A woman who appears to be alone asks if you mind if she takes the seat next to you. Sensing what appears to be an unhappy countenance, you choose to initiate cordial conversation. The conversation takes on a more serious tone when you ask about her family. She tearfully discloses how uptight she has become since her aunt, an elderly widow with no children of her own, has come to live with them (a family of four—two adults and two children) indefinitely while rehabilitating from a major stroke. Launching out on a business adventure she had held in her dreams for so long would have to be put on hold due to the personal care needed for her sick aunt and home alterations made to accommodate her. "She interferes. She is constantly giving unsolicited instruction of how to be a good Christian wife, mother, and homemaker—things I already know! Sometimes family plans and outings have to be readjusted. The children daily look forward to the jovial demeanor of their aunt. I really care about her, but this just doesn't seem fair. It was not supposed to be like this. Our lives have been turned upside down." She shares she has somewhat reluctantly looked into several convalescent facilities to eliminate the burden and inconvenience. Perhaps this was the answer. What would you tell your new friend?

CHAPTER 10

Home Management

*G*ood home management is an outgrowth of dedicated personal management. In Titus 2:3–5, home management is the primary role of the wife. Christian women are instructed:

TO BE (character): Character determines conduct	TO DO (conduct): Conduct reflects character
kind	busy at home
lover of her own husband	subject to her own husband
lover of her children	teacher of what is good
self-controlled	not a slanderer
pure	
reverent	

The following are helpful tools that will develop or sharpen your home management skills. Some of the tools that will enhance the order and supervision of your life, family and home are setting priorities and goals, scheduling, using a calendar, constructing a daily to do list, grocery shopping, and budgeting your finances. Pray and ask the Lord for wisdom as you adopt these tools that will bring structure and balance to your life, family, and home (James 1:5–8).

SETTING PRIORITIES

We tend to settle on one of three extremes regarding life's choices. Either we are everywhere accomplishing little, we let life just happen, or we refuse to venture from our nice structure. Establishing priorities helps us focus. Having structure based on set priorities is a necessary means for fulfilling our responsibilities and setting goals in line with God's revealed will. Always keep before you that God is in control. We are simply the managers of what He has entrusted to us, which is not much when we think about what He is responsible for. Yet He maintains order. WOW!

A priority list will help you to identify what is important to God. After praying for wisdom (Proverbs 3:6, 16:9):

1. Identify the major components of your life by asking yourself, "What am I?" (I am . . . a woman,

a Christian, a wife, a mother, single, a widow, a single-parent etc.)
2. Search the Scriptures to determine what God says are the responsibilities in each of these areas.
3. Then place those responsibilities under their corresponding title.

Now you have a basic structure for organizing your life and family in accordance with God's will. See Sample-HM-1 in the back of the book to help you.

SETTING GOALS

A goal can be defined as a predetermined end to be accomplished at a predetermined time (Job 42:2; Psalm 33:11; Proverbs 14:22; 16:1–3; 20:18; Isaiah 32:8). These goals may fall into the following categories: spiritual, physical, mental, social, and financial.

Write down one goal from each category that you would like to accomplish by the end of the year. Some of your goals will and should include development in the areas from your priority list. Remember the key is WHAT GOD WANTS. Start small. As you make progress, you will gain hope. Another key is consistency. The following is a sample of goals for each of the categories. The details listed are just a few ideas. These can be used or you may come up with your own.

A. Spiritual Goals (Relationship with God)

IDEAS:

1. Read through the Bible.
2. Witness to one person a month (Purchase the booklet, "Four Spiritual Laws").
3. Commit to regular church worship, Sunday School, and Bible study attendance.
4. Commit to a regular time for prayer and meditation of Scripture. There can be a different concentration for prayer each day.
Sunday - Praise and adoration to the Lord
Monday - Immediate family members and family goals
Tuesday - Extended family members, unsaved family members, and neighbors
Wednesday - Leadership at home, church, city, state, and country
Thursday - Missionaries from your congregation
Friday - Sick & shut-in from your congregation
Saturday - Your personal life

After one year has gone by, evaluate your progress. Do not get distracted by what someone else is reading and studying. Start where you are and remain diligent. Soon you will have experience, knowledge, and spiritual faith muscle behind you. Now you can set further goals. Remember to pray for wisdom and to watch your development. God will do it (Psalm 139: 23–24)! Remember the formula from chapter one?

The Word of God + personal application in faith = spiritual growth

Spiritual growth + spiritual growth = spiritual maturity and intimacy with Christ

Now that you have read through the Bible, you may want to begin the process of applying what you have learned. After praying, pick four areas for the year. Your aim can be one area per quarter. Perhaps there are hindrances you want to begin working through. What does the Bible say about the hindrance or area of sin you have chosen to work on? When working on areas of hindrances, weaknesses or sin, do not become overwhelmed. We will be ever-changing until the day we die. Even then, our greatest change will be putting off mortality for immortality. Sometimes working on one area will automatically eradicate another area. Trusting God and remembering His love and commitment to you is paramount. Be sensitive to the Holy Spirit. He will guide you in identifying God's will for you at a given time. Remember that the key is *intimacy* with the *Lord*, not works. You may utilize the following schedule to help you develop a system for studying and applying God's Word.

> Sunday - Praise and adoration to the Lord
> Monday - Study sermon notes
> Tuesday - Church Bible study lesson
> Wednesday - Sunday school lesson
> Thursday - Area of personal growth
> Friday - Old Testament passage
> Saturday - New Testament passage

B. Physical Goals - Remember start small. Choose 1 or 2 for the year. Then build on them the following years.

IDEAS:

1. Lose weight - 2 lbs. a month = 24 lbs. for the year.
2. Exercise 5 to 10 minutes daily or 15 to 30 minutes every other day.
3. Wash your hair weekly.
4. Go to the dentist (for good dental hygiene we should visit our dentist regularly every 6 months).
5. Go to the gynecologist (have a mammogram).
6. Paint your nails once a week.

C. Mental Goals - Remember to start small. Pick one.

IDEAS:

1. Sign up for tutoring if you cannot read or do not read well.
2. If you do not like to read, select a small book on a topic you enjoy or want to learn more about.
3. Read the newspaper once a week or one column a day.
4. Go to the library once a month.
5. Discipline your mind to think more rather than live by your emotions.
6. Memorize one Scripture per week.
7. Take a computer class at your local community college or high school that offers evening classes for the community.

D. Social Goals - Remember to start small. God loves people, and we want to be imitators of Christ. You may not have any trouble being social—so much so that you do not always get to your responsibilities. If this is the case, here are a few suggestions.

IDEAS:

1. Talk to close friends only once or twice a week.

2. Meet the neighbors on both sides and across the street.
3. Keep telephone conversations to 10 minutes.
4. Schedule time out each month with a girl-friend or with the girls.
5. Set goals for the relationships with individuals in your home.
6. *COURT EVERY MEMBER OF YOUR FAMILY. THEY'RE WORTH IT!*

   a. Spouse: Where is the relationship now?
   Where do you see it going?
   Where do you want it to go?
   Where does the Bible say it should be?
   What will you do to effect change?

   IDEAS:

   1. Measure where the relationship is now spiritually, mentally, physically, and emotionally.
   2. Set your most immediate goal where the relationship is weak.
   3. Set a goal in at least one area.
   4. The key is CONSISTENCY.
   5. Be watchful in determining goals with your mate. What does he complain about most or what things do you do that make his face look funny?

6. Read at least one marriage book a year.

b. Children: Go through the same process with each individual child. Keep a folder on each child.

IDEAS:

1. Add their abilities, what they like to do and places they like to go to your list of goals (Philippians 2:3–4).
2. Read at least (1) parenting book a year.

c. Friends: Also, go through the same process for close friends or building a close friendship. Negate those areas that may not be applicable.

SCHEDULING

A schedule is a set time in which to carry out your daily and weekly responsibilities both inside and outside of the home. In doing so, we make the most of our time, and reach our predetermined goals (Ephesians 5:15–16).

Now that you have set goals, the next step is to compose a schedule to implement those goals. Make it realistic. In order to do this, you would need to monitor the time it takes to get a specific job done effectively when you are well. The time will not be the same during your menstrual showing or an illness. Give yourself more time during these intervals.

A. Your schedule should include: (See Sample-HM-2a/2b)

1. Daily and weekly responsibilities
2. Worship, Sunday School, Bible study
3. Reflection of goals
4. A rest day from routine
5. Outside family activities
6. Space and time for travel
7. A daily rest period (tea-time)

A personal schedule can be composed using the blank form found on page HM-2d.
SPECIAL NOTES:

1. Give yourself three weeks to adjust to your new schedule, adding items as you go. By week four you should be able to make adjustments and additions if needed.
2. If you are home when the children come home from school, one half-hour before they arrive, close out what you are doing to get mentally prepared for their arrival. You may

want to have some snacks prepared and avoid all incoming calls at this time.

3. If you are a working mom, leave the issues of the day at work. During your drive or ride home, rest and prepare your mind for ministering to your family. If necessary, train your family to grab a snack of their choice for the first half-hour that you are home. That will diminish their hunger pains and allow you some extra time to get refreshed privately in your room. They can also read a book or play quietly in their room until you have had time to regroup.

4. Send the members of your family off in the morning full, happy, and prayed over.

B. Prepare a schedule for each child. Teenagers can prepare their own schedules with supervision. Their schedule should include: (See Sample-HM-2c)

Chores (daily & weekly)	Reading
Responsibilities	Eating
(daily & weekly)	(meals & snacks)
School hours	Bathing
Homework	Play & Exercise
Outside activities	Church worship
Sleep	Daily devotional time
Rest	Reflection of goals

CALENDAR

A calendar is a helpful aid in short and long-term planning. It provides the means to see the overall picture of activity of our lives and in the life of our family.

Two types of calendars are needed: a pocket-sized one for your handbag and a regular wall calendar for the family. For planning purposes, it is prudent to stay three months ahead on the family calendar.

Both calendars should include the following: (See Sample-HM-3a and Form-HM-3b)

1. Husband's appointments - Doctor/work/car/guys
   Children's appointments - Doctor/dentist/barber
   Personal appointments - Doctor/hair/girls
2. Church activities - Worship/Sunday School/Bible study/special events
3. Birthdays - Immediate family, general family, friends
4. Grocery Day/shopping days for family (clothes & shoes)
5. Pay days
6. Holidays
7. Purchases - major (car & appliances) and minor (cards for birthday and get-well)
8. Home projects
9. Eating out

Home Management

DAILY THINGS-TO-DO LIST

A daily things-to-do list is a list of responsibilities to be completed on a given day. This list can be made by writing down the activities from your schedule and calendar. Pray for God to order your steps. The following should be considered when preparing this list: (See Sample-HM-4a and Form-HM-4b)

1. Are there items that can be completed simultaneously?
2. How many telephone calls need to be made?
3. How many are in-house items? How many items have to be completed outside the home?
4. Add to the list any items that come up that are not on your calendar or schedule.
5. Evaluate any items not mentioned on the calendar and the schedule by asking the daily priority questions listed below. Then number the items on your list in order of priority.
6. Proceed to follow your schedule.
7. Trust the Lord for items not completed. Put them on the list for the next day or the following week.
8. Thank the Lord for a day well spent.

Questions of Daily Priority

Throughout the course of a day, urgent and unexpected events are bound to come up. How do you handle them in light of what is on your daily things to do list? Establishing daily priorities involves asking ourselves a few questions that help us determine what is most important at a given time. This principle is also effective when, establishing goals, designing the calendar, composing our schedules, making out our grocery list, and considering our budget.

Ask yourself the following questions, be flexible and remember that prayer is a vital tool:

1. Does the urgent or unexpected have a set time that it has to be completed?
2. What will be hindered if the unexpected is not completed immediately?
3. Can the unexpected demand or request be worked into my schedule for the day? If so, how will it affect my normal routine?
4. What can be altered from my regular routine that can wait without consequences due to procrastination or neglect?
5. Can the unexpected be placed on my schedule for another time with a reasonable and timely deadline?
6. Does the urgent involve a fellow human being? Is it life or death? Has the person who needs me had the problem for a long time? If a person comes to you with a long-standing problem they want to discuss with you immediately, take the time to lovingly give the person hope and Scripture. Then you may suggest a time when

you can get together with them to discuss the problem in more detail. Their problem did not arise overnight and it won't be resolved overnight. If you are concerned that your responsibilities will not allow you to give them the adequate time and attention they need, see if they are open to share with another trustworthy individual you recommend.

7. If a person calls on you for help and their problem is due to their neglect and irresponsibility, be willing to help and show mercy. Then kindly suggest how they might handle it in the future. If you notice a pattern developing, i.e., they continue to be neglectful and dependent on you to rescue them, be kind, and inform them that you can no longer render services under the present circumstances. Use Scripture to help them see truth. Then pray with them and for them.

Christ demonstrated the principle of priority throughout His stay on earth:

1. When Satan was in the wilderness tempting Christ, He refused to misuse His power as God. He had come to earth to die for man; He remained focused despite temptation.

2. When Christ came to John the Baptist to be baptized, John initially refused. But Christ let him know that it must be in order to fulfill all things. He remained focused despite opposition.

3. Lazarus, Jesus' friend, died and had been dead for four days before Christ came to the scene in order that others would see God's glory. Christ remained focused despite urgency and the crowd.

4. Christ refused to come down off of the cross to save Himself, knowing that we needed a Savior. His goal was always to do the Father's will. He remained focused despite brutal persecution.

GROCERIES

A very vital component to home management is maintaining a reasonable supply of food and supplies. The following guidelines will help you to achieve this goal.

1. Determine the breakfast, lunch and dinner menu for the next week, two weeks, or month, depending on your grocery schedule (See Sample-HM-5a and Form-HM-5b). This will determine exactly what food items are needed. Eat healthy! Pray for wisdom.

2. Prepare a food budget—a pre-planned dollar amount for food and supplies.

3. Type out a permanent grocery list in store aisle order or according to food groups and make copies. Thus, there is no need to start from scratch each time. You may utilize the grocery list in the back of the book (for non-commercial use only). (See Form-HM-6).

4. Estimate the cost to determine how much money you will need, then total.

5. Purchase the Sunday paper for coupons. Cut them out and categorize them in a coupon filing system.

6. After determining the cost of your groceries, identify the coupons to be used. For additional savings, shop at wholesale stores.

7. Pray before going shopping. God may cause someone to drop the coupon you need or allow sales on items you do not have coupons for.

8. Save receipt(s) for 30 days.

9. Shop at stores where the freshest foods are available, coupons are doubled, and personal bagging is optional.

10. Purchase in bulk only when the space and financial resources are available. Sometimes finances are limited. Be a wise shopper and remember God will supply your every need.

11. Keep some money aside to replace milk, fruit, and bread if freezing is not an option.

12. Increase your food budget yearly with increase in the economy.

13. Consider healthy meal stretchers: chili, homemade soups (chicken and turkey noodle), beans and rice.

BUDGETING

God has called us to be good and faithful stewards of what He has given us (Luke 16:1–13). A practical way to achieve this is to set up and follow a monthly budget. The goal of a monthly budget is to help prevent our family from spending more than it makes. It may take awhile to get used to a budget if you are not already using one. But with diligence, determination and prayer, you can not only adhere to a budget, but ultimately experience financial freedom. The following list can be used as a guideline or starting point for setting up a family budget.

A. MONTHLY BUDGET (See Form-HM-7).

1. Make an itemized list of all fixed monthly expenditures.

    a. Place your tithe at the top of the list (10% of monthly gross income).
    b. Second from the top, set aside your savings (4% of monthly gross income).
    c. List the monthly payment of debts owed.
    d. List irregular expenditures such as bi-monthly, quarterly, six months or yearly expenses.
        (You may want to break these expenditures down to a monthly cost so they do not require a large sum of money at one time.)
    e. Total the cost of the monthly expenditures.

2. List monthly income.

    a. your income

    b. your mate's income

    c. When married, it is God's will that the income of both spouses be combined and placed in a joint account to which both parties have access.

3. Subtract the monthly expenditures from the monthly income. Your monthly income should exceed your monthly expenditures.

B. SETTING UP THE BUDGET FOR MONTHLY PROCESSING

1. On a sheet of paper or by computer, list monthly expenditures on the left-hand side.

2. Try to divide your expenditures according to your pay schedule. If payment is weekly still divide the expenditures so that bills are paid on the 15th and 30th of the month. Determine what day the bills are due by looking on the bill for the due date. Any bill due between the 20th and the 4th, you pay on the 15th of the month. Any bill due between the 5th and 19th, pay on the 30th of the month. Thus you can avoid late fees, unless you have made special arrangements with the creditor.

3. On the right-hand side of the paper, make two columns: one for the 15th and one for the 30th.
4. Proceed down the list of expenditures and identify the due date, then the monthly cost. List the monthly cost under the appropriate date according to the scale in item #2.
5. Total your expenditures for the 15th. Total your expenditures for the 30th.
6. Be sure there is money in your bank to cover each cost.

C. WEEKLY/MONTHLY/QUARTERLY REPORT (See Form-HM-8)

1. 4 weekly reports make up your monthly report.
2. 3 monthly reports make up your quarterly report.
3. Attach receipts in your expense envelope and remaining cash from the envelope to weekly reports.
4. Turn in a financial record of actual spending from the previous quarter to your husband.
5. Make request for funds for upcoming quarter. Predetermine financial needs by:

   a. Looking on the calendar for planned activities that incur a cost.
   b. Determining weekly, monthly, and quarterly cost of activities.

6. Submit report to spouse for approval and modification at which time it should be measured against your fixed budget, which includes your monthly income, savings, and fixed expenditures.

7. Upon approval and finalizing of your quarterly budget, stick to your paperwork. Do not give in to the lust of the eye and or the pride of life, nor try and keep up with your neighbor. Ignore the temptation to give off false messages of where you stand financially as a family.

More Financial Wisdom

If your family's personal finances are limited, pray for God's wisdom. God will show you what to forgo, what to put on hold, and what purchases can be made to give hope. He will also show you what your family should keep as an expenditure and what to trust the Lord to provide by faith.

If your family is financially comfortable, i.e., all of your needs are met and there is a surplus at the end of each month, do not be quick to change your lifestyle nor spend large portions of your surplus on perishable items such as a new top-of-the-line car, food or clothing. There are no tax advantages to purchasing a new car, and items like food and clothing are perishable items that satisfy only for the moment. Pray and ask God to show you exactly what He wants you to do with the surplus. Here are a few suggestions:

1. Become debt-free
2. Increase savings
3. Plan for a family vacation
4. Invest resources in real estate, mutual funds and money market accounts
5. Plan for the children's college tuition
6. Save for retirement
7. Plan and pay for burial plots
8. Support missionaries
9. Increase giving to others

Make it a practice to make all purchases with cash, an American Express Card or the like, in order to avoid building debt. Predetermine what purchases will be made with the American Express Card and subtract that amount from the bank balance to ensure that the money is in the bank when the monthly American Express statement is due. When making a major purchase, research to identify the best quality at a cost that is affordable.

Purchasing a pocket expense divider is a good way to keep money for various expenditures separate. Take money out of the bank by the week, and not the full month. Avoid taking more into the store than you need. Do not spend change from purchases or add it to another purchase without documentation. Replace cash with a receipt in the envelope. Deposit any remaining cash into your checking or savings account. Hold and file receipts for major purchases for at least 7 years.

PRAYER

Dear Lord,

From A Personal Profile to Home Management, I have learned principles that when followed will bless my life. Working through *A Personal Profile*, I learned to live a Christ-centered life. As I moved through *The Christian Woman's Identity*, I learned just how much You love me and that that love is the anchor for my self-esteem and will in turn free me to love You and others unselfishly. While *Biblical Blueprints of the Christian Woman* showed me Your revealed will for me and examples of women in the Bible who carried it out, *The Christian Woman's Sexual Conduct* took me a step further. I obtained a close view of your will for me and my biblical and physical responsibility to honor You with my body. The Virtuous Woman put it all together with a most excellent and motivating portrayal of the Christian woman who made God's principles her heart and life priority. Now it is my turn. I was challenged in *Taking Personal Responsibility for Your Life* that my life is a gift from You and it is my responsibility to make it count. *Personal Management* taught me Your will for me to manage what You have entrusted to me and how to practically do so. As I ventured on to *Overthrowing Life's Hindrances and Sin*, I became strengthened in my faith to address sin and weak areas of my life. In You I learned that I can overcome and not be controlled by the hindrances and sins that have held me captive. Then *The Grace of Humility* helped me see myself in relationship to You and my neighbor. I learned that when I reverence You and love my neighbor I have a proper view of myself. With all of this, I feel I am ready and equipped to manage my family and my home with the tools I received from *Home Management*.

Lord, be with me as I set out to make Your priorities for me, my priorities, and as I set goals to accomplish them. Grant our family grace as I devise a calendar that encompasses each of our lives. Help me to set schedules for the children and grant me the strength to ensure that they stick to them. Order my steps each day as I put together my Daily Things-To-Do List and the bi-monthly dinner menu. Help me to exercise discipline over our finances while making small purchases like the groceries, as well as planning for large ones. Lord, I am quite excited about putting the proper order in place for the success of my family and home. I pray that each member is blessed and that You are glorified as we align our lives with You.

SCENARIO, "MISMANAGED"

After dropping the children off at school, as normal, you gather with the other moms for some small talk. Your heads turn at the sound of tires and doors slamming, but you resume your conversation. It is only Debbie pulling up in front of the school, tardy, as is her custom. Her children dash out of the car and into school. Your children often complain about the disruption Debbie's kids are in class and question their wrinkled clothing and lack of personal grooming. Debbie approaches the group and divulges that rather than walking with the group this morning, she was going to scurry home to down the left over pizza from dinner last night and head for bed. Debbie is overweight and frequently in the condition she is this morning. You pray silently in your heart about what God would have you to do. While the women in the group continue talking, you walk Debbie to her car. What will you say?

CHAPTER 11

Hurdling Stress

Stress is the emotional and physical state that results from the mind's response to life's circumstances. It is the body's reaction to difficult, adverse and hard to process information or circumstances. We tell ourselves, "I can't take it," or "I can't handle it." We stand somewhere between it being thrust upon us and not wanting it, not knowing what to do with it and not knowing how or when it will be handled. We want it resolved NOW and our mind, body and our emotions validate that verdict.

Many of life's circumstances and conditions can become potential stress factors, i.e., sources that can lead to stress. Whether or not these factors result in the manifestation of stress depends upon our perspective and response to them. Oftentimes the root of stress factors can be a result of our negligence or poor decisions.

There are times when other people or circumstances beyond our control can also be the source. The Christian woman encounters many potential stress factors on a regular basis.

POTENTIAL STRESS FACTORS FOR WOMEN

- A crying baby
- A rebellious teen
- Poor life management
- Being over-worked
- Sickness (handicap)
- Financial deficiencies
- Poor marriage relationship (lack of communications and/or leadership)
- Living with individuals with varying temperaments and personalities
- Lack of wisdom and knowledge of God's Word
- Unconfessed sin or disobedience to God
- Physical changes (i.e., menstrual cycle, PMS, menopause and aging)

Isn't it interesting that the further we move away from God, the more sensitive we become regarding us and our circumstances? The more sickness there is? Not relying on God or not acknowledging God limits us to our natural and finite knowledge and abilities, so much so that when life deals us more than we can handle, the result is a sense of hopelessness or distress.

Having an unbiblical view of our circumstances can lead to an unbiblical response.

SOME UNBIBLICAL RESPONSES TO STRESS FACTORS

Stress Factors	Unbiblical Responses
• A crying baby	• Impatience and anger: yelling at, hitting or spanking the baby and taking our frustration out on others
• Over-worked	• Short with others, self-pity
• Sickness (short-term, handicap, terminal)	• Push beyond limits, self-pity, fear
• Financial deficiencies	• Debt (credit cards), stealing, coveting, envy, gambling or illegal gain, daydreaming, self-pity
• Poor marriage relationship (lack of communications and/or leadership)	• Divorce, adultery, reversal of roles, insubordination, disrespect, retreat, independence

215

- Living with individuals with varying temperaments and personalities

- Non-acceptance, conditional love, derogation, mockery, slander

- Lack of wisdom and knowledge of the Bible

- Seek advice from the unsaved and ungodly, live by emotions, the mind of the old nature or intuition

- Unconfessed sin and disobedience

- Continuance in known sin (rebellion and stubbornness) and disobedience, ignoring the prompting of the Holy Spirit and/or admonishment

- Procrastination

- Make excuses, do busy work rather than meet responsibilities, increase social relationships to quiet convictions or meeting responsibilities

- Physical changes (menstrual cycle, PMS, menopause, aging)

- Depression, self-centeredness, lashing out, blame-shifting, denial

- Poor life management (physical, emotional, mental, psychological, spiritual, social, financial)

- Allowing people, circumstances, and emotions to dictate choices rather than God's Word and our responsibility to God

- Rebellious teens

- Self-righteousness, impatience, permissiveness, fear, unforgiveness, lack of commitment (relinquishing parental responsibility, or inappropriate punishment)

217

If the stress factors in a Christian woman's life are not handled appropriately on a consistent basis, they lead to bigger problems and increase our chances for stress. Stress can manifest itself mentally, emotionally, and physically.

WHAT STRESS CAN LOOK LIKE

Mental manifestation

- Instability
- Stuck
- Depression
- Worry
- Confusion/Disoriented

Emotional manifestation

- Anxiety
- Turmoil
- A lack of peace and rest
- Overwhelmed
- Fear
- Nervousness

Physical - Short-term outward manifestation

- Hives
- Isolation
- Curtness

- Outburst
- Nervousness
- Tiredness
- Busyness
- Impatience
- Unkempt
- Blurred vision
- Sickness
- Tight Chest
- Overeating or loss of appetite
- Headaches
- Alcohol or substance abuse

Physical - Long-term outward manifestation

- Physical illness
- High blood pressure
- Heart disease
- Obesity
- Diabetes

A SOLUTION FOR STRESS

We can manage the degree to which we allow ourselves to be consumed by stress. A Christian woman who chooses to hurdle and outlive stress must: 1) be willing to acknowledge that stress is a sign for change and should not be a normal way of life, 2) be honest about her state, situation, or condition, 3) evaluate her behavior and choices, and most importantly, 4) come to the Lord.

Stress

Our perspective and response to difficult or hard to handle information, situations, or circumstances can turn what initially began as a potential and isolated stress factor into anger, worry, or fear. If allowed to persist, these will fester into wrong thinking that affects our choices, our behavior and ultimately, our health. Jesus admonishes the believer not to worry, but to embrace His peace and to be encouraged because He had overcome the world (John 14:1,27; 16:33). Jesus is our anchor and hope. As children of God, we are MORE THAN conquerors no matter what comes our way internationally, nationally, regionally, locally, or personally.

Honesty about our state

God will use various sources to bring us to the reality of our state: the man of God (the preacher, pastor, or elder), a close relative, a loving friend, a stranger, our health, or our circumstances. Identify, if you can, the source of your stress. What is bothering you and why? Make a itemized list of every situation, condition, circumstance, or person that fosters anger, worry, or fear within you. You may have a long list or you may have only one or two items on your list. Writing them down relieves the mind and ultimately our bodies of the stress and strain we place on them. Writing them down also places distance between the issue(s) and us. Our minds become free to think rationally. Likewise, when we are honest about our state, the situation becomes a little easier to address. Next, identify whether your situation is short-term, long-term, or life-long.

Evaluation of behavior and choices

Addressing and evaluating the cause of your stress may require help from a close objective family member (a Christian), a mature Christian friend, or Christian counselor. If we are the source of our stress, (negligence, poor decisions, inappropriate behavior, bad attitude, etc.) we must confess our sin to God, and then repent of that sin by turning to God and away from our sin. If our sin is a bad habit that has been practiced over time, when we confess and repent of our sin, God will forgive us immediately. Regarding our condition, God may deliver us out of our state immediately or He may choose to have us work through our situation as He did the children of Israel when Pharaoh let them go and they began their journey for the Promise Land. He did so because He knew they were not strong enough for war and to teach them to depend on Him for the necessities of life (Exodus 13:17; 15:23–25). Either way, we can rest assure that His grace will accompany us. Once we have repented of our sin, we are back in fellowship with God; we are at peace with God (Romans 5:1) and have the peace of God (Philippians 4:7).

Turn to the Lord

Turning to the Lord is our hope and certainty for change (Matthew 11:28–29; Deuteronomy 33:27). We must turn to Jesus in prayer and ask Him to show us His way of dealing with our circumstances. When you find yourself overwhelmed by life's circumstances or troubled, as previously mentioned, write all of your concerns down on paper one by one. In writing them on paper, you get them out of your head and heart, to give them to Jesus. Then you can release them to Him through prayer. A simple, "Lord, I give this over to You," is all you have to say. As a visible sign of releasing your cares to Jesus, you can burn the list, bury it, tear the list to shreds and throw it away. This step will also be your stake in the ground to remind you of your change when the devil attempts to confuse you by bringing it up again. You may also choose to keep the list in your Bible, journal or wherever you spend time for prayer. In doing so, you can continue to keep it before the Lord in prayer. Refuse to entertain the items in your mind like a scratched CD, but rather address them in faith with the wisdom God gives, making sure that after you have followed God's instructions regarding your situation, that you leave it with God.

If your stress is caused by circumstances beyond your control or people outside of yourself, it is possible for your circumstances to be short-term, long-term, or life-long. But as God told Paul when he pleaded with the Lord to take his condition away, "My grace is sufficient for you, for my power is made perfect in weakness" (2 Corinthians 12:9). As you turn to God in your circumstances, He will change you and/or your circumstances, give you peace and direction under unchanged circumstances, give you wisdom and grace to change your circumstances, or give you strength to bear your circumstances.

Ask yourself, "What is God's will and what does God want to develop in me as a result of my circumstances?" The Lord is very interested in us. He is able to sustain us through any situation. He will allow our circumstances to linger or remain until His will is complete in us.

But we must be willing to change (Romans 8:28–32; James 1:4). Let us look at some biblical models.

BIBLICAL EXAMPLES

Woman with the Issue of Blood (Matthew 9:20–22; Luke 8:43–48; Mark 5:25–34)

Stress factor (beyond her control): She had been sick for twelve years; the doctors could not heal her.

What she did: She spent all she had on medical care.

God factor: She reached out to touch Jesus by faith.

Result: She was instantly healed, Jesus pronounced that her faith made her well.

Martha (Luke 10:38–41; John 12:1–3)

Stress factor (by choice): Overworked, mixed priorities.

What she did: Distressed over sister's lack of participation, complained to Jesus.

God factor: Jesus admonished Martha to right her priorities, to listen to Him.

Result: The next time Martha served, she had no anxiety, but was a gracious host.

Hannah - (1 Samuel 1 & 2)

Stress factor (beyond her control): Childless; taunted by Peninnah, her husband's other wife (who had children)

What she did: Wept and would not eat (she was anguished and grieved); Hannah went to the LORD's temple and poured her soul out to the LORD.

God factor: The man of God (Eli) spoke a blessing upon Hannah.

Result: Hannah conceived Samuel; she dedicated Samuel to the LORD; Samuel became God's prophet and God gave Hannah more children.

King David (2 Samuel 11 & 12 and Psalm 51)

Stress factor (by choice): King David committed adultery against God and with Uriah's wife, Bathsheba.

What he did: David had Uriah murdered to cover over his sin of adultery then David married Bathsheba.

God factor: God sent Nathan, the man of God, to confront King David.

Result: David repented of his sins and his fellowship with God was restored. David had to live with the consequences of his sin and was chastised by God; God took the life of the baby conceived through David and Bathsheba's adulterous act. Because David committed murder, God said that the sword would not depart from his house. David would experience calamity from within his own house and God would cause someone close to David to openly sleep with his wives. God gave David and Bathsheba another son, Solomon whom God claimed as His son.

David and Martha's stress stemmed from their ungodly attitude, choices and behavior. The source of stress for the woman with the issue of blood and Hannah was beyond their control. While the sources of stress varied for each, the common means of overcoming the stress was God. The Lord is our hope for change. "Come to me, all you who are weary and burdened, and I will give you rest. Take my yoke upon you and learn from me, for I am gentle and humble in heart, and you will find rest for your souls. For my yoke is easy and my burden is light" (Matthew 11:28–29).

HURDLING STRESS WITH PEACE

The moment we step out of bed, anything in this world can become a potential stress factor if we allow it

(John 16:33). But Jesus left the believer His peace (John 14:27). It is ours to embrace. The Christian woman cannot obtain peace from any source other than Christ. Peace is resting in God's will. Maintaining that peace is doing God's will and focusing on Christ, regardless of the nature of our circumstances. We cannot fix our circumstances on our own, in the flesh, according to our will and desires. We have to be willing to wait on the Lord (Psalm 27:14).

A lack of peace can stem from a divided mind. A divided mind is the result of: (1) a lack of mental control, (2) dwelling on wrong thoughts, (3) intrusive thoughts of Satan, (4) incorrect mental responses to life's difficulties (attitude), (5) not nourishing the mind with God's Word, (6) not believing and appropriating God's Word in faith, (7) not getting enough physical rest, and (8) a lack of trust in God's ability to do what He has promised. As a Christian woman submits to God, she can be confident that He will deliver His way and in His time. Romans 5:5 says hope does not disappoint because the Holy Spirit whom God has given us pours out God's love into our hearts. When we come to Him with our cares, He comforts our hearts. When we entrust our cares to Him, He gives us peace of mind. "You will keep in perfect peace him whose mind is steadfast, because he trusts in you" (Isaiah 26:3).

HURDLING STRESS THROUGH FAITH

"The righteous will live by faith" (Romans 1:17). I have been redeemed (bought back) by the blood of

Jesus Christ and declared righteous (justification). As a result of this transaction, I have everything I need for godliness, but even more, I have been transferred from the kingdom of darkness into God's marvelous kingdom of light. I am a Christian, a believer. As a Christian, I live by a new way. My perspective is no longer limited to me, but through a right relationship with God through Christ, my life has taken on a new dimension. I now live my life by faith in the God who saved me, namely Jesus Christ. "I have been crucified with Christ and I no longer live, but Christ lives in me. The life I live in the body, I live by faith in the Son of God, who loved me and gave Himself for me" (Galatians 2:20).

The Scriptures say that Enoch, who lived 365 years, became the father of Methuselah (the oldest man to ever live) and walked with God. The Bible says, "then he was no more, because God took him away" (Genesis 5:21–24). When we reference this passage to Hebrews 11:6, we find out that Enoch was a man of faith. Walking with God requires faith.

Faith is being sure of what we hope for and certain of what we do not see (Hebrews 11:1). Faith requires a new way of thinking. It is having a new attitude! FAITH is believing as though it is done. Let us take the earth for example. Scripture confirms that what we see was not made by what is visible. "By faith we understand that the universe was formed at God's command, so that what is seen was not made out of what was visible" (Hebrews 11:3). Now make sure you get this—something does not have to materialize before we believe it. The fact that God is . . . is what makes it so. That is why the Scripture says, "And without faith it is impossible to please God, because anyone who comes to him must believe that he exists and that he rewards those who earnestly seek him" (Hebrews 11:6). Faith dictates believing God (believing what is not as though it is), standing on that belief and exercising God confidence.

Faith in action invokes the grace and power of God. Hebrews 11:2 states, "This is what the ancients were commended for." Hebrews 11:5 speaks of Enoch thusly, "he was commended as one who pleased God." To commend means to entrust for care or preservation, to recommend as worthy of confidence or notice, to mention with approbation or praise. In short, commend means to reward. God gets excited when we exercise faith in Him. Consider how excited we get when our children trust and obey us. They should obey us in obedience to God, but the truth of the matter is that obedience is a choice. They could either choose to obey or disobey. When children obey, they have made a conscious choice to do so. As a result we are blessed.

In our home, we celebrate the smallest things. For example, the other day I received a call from my youngest son who is a freshman in college. He ran for the office of a Judge. We prayed and asked the Lord to continue to honor and validate what our son believes is God's will for his life. God honored our prayers and he was elected to the Judge seat. When he called home, he said he was excited, but knew that when he told his friends at school they would just say, "Congratulations." He said, "Mom, I'm used to celebrating. If I were at home, we'd celebrate." He knew that as a family we do not just get excited, but in our excitement we celebrate the person's achievement and honor God for His blessings! That is exactly how God gets when we exercise faith. God will put our faith on display. He may grant the devil permission to bring trouble into our lives. First of all God knows that we have faith in Him and it is through that "trouble" He will grow our faith. Secondly, He is in control and an ever-present help in our time of need.

Hebrews hallmarks the faith of the prophet Daniel. In Daniel chapter 6, King Darius set satraps to rule throughout his kingdom. He set administrators over the satraps, one of whom was Daniel. Because of Daniel's excellent qualities, King Darius purposed in his heart to promote Daniel over the entire kingdom. When the other administrators became aware of it, they became jealous and set out to ambush Daniel in order to make Daniel look bad before the king. They sought to find fault in his work. They could not. Scripture says that Daniel was not corrupt or negligent, but was trustworthy. So the administrators set a trap to ensnare Daniel against the king. They had the king order a decree that would place Daniel in opposition with the king's edict or in opposition to Daniel's allegiance to God. For thirty days no one was to pray to any god or man except the king.

It was Daniel's practice to pray a prayer of thanksgiving to God three times in a day. The king was informed of what appeared to be defiance by Daniel and with reluctance, was forced to carry out his own decree of placing Daniel in the lions' den. The next morning the king hurried to see if God had delivered Daniel. To the king's delight, Daniel remained untouched and unharmed by the lions. The king had Daniel lifted from the den and had Daniel's accusers and their families thrown into the lions' den. They were devoured before ever reaching the floor of the den. God not only shut the mouths of the lions, but He punished the men who set out to destroy Daniel. King Darius then issued another decree that in every part of his kingdom the people must fear and reverence the God of Daniel.

> *Be self-controlled and alert. Your enemy the devil prowls around like a roaring lion looking for someone to devour. Resist him, standing firm in the faith, because you know that your brothers throughout the world are undergoing the same kind of sufferings. And the God of all grace, who called you to his eternal glory in Christ, after you have suffered a little while, will himself restore you and make you strong, firm and steadfast. To him be the power for ever and ever. Amen (1 Peter 5:8–11).*

On what grounds was God willing to be Daniel's judge and deliverer? God placed Daniel in his royal position and no one but God could remove him (6:1). Daniel took personal responsibility for his job. He performed his job so well that the king wanted to promote him by setting him over his entire kingdom (6:3). Daniel was trustworthy, neither corrupt nor negligent. Daniel was faithful to God (6:4). Daniel prayed three times in a day, giving thanks to God. Daniel did not honor the king above God (6:10, 20). Daniel trusted God while being persecuted. He did not retaliate. Daniel did not compromise or shrink back in his faith (6:16, 23). Daniel honored the king (6:21). Daniel had a godly reputation before God and man (6:20, 22). God was willing to be Daniel's judge (6:22). God delivered Daniel (6:23). God prospered Daniel (6:28).

> *"And what more shall I say? I do not have time to tell about Gideon, Barak, Samson, Jephthah, David, Samuel and the prophets, who through faith conquered kingdoms, administered justice, and gained what was promised; who shut the mouths of lions, quenched the fury of the flames, and escaped the edge of the sword, whose weakness was turned to strength; and who became powerful in battle and routed foreign armies. Women received back their dead, raised to life again. Others were torture and refused to be released, so that they might gain a better resurrection. Some faced jeers and floggings, while still others were chained and put in prison. They were stoned, they were sawed in two, they were put to death by the sword. They went about in sheepskins and goatskins, destitute, persecuted, and mistreated" (Hebrews 11:32–37).*

Through all of their trials, conditions, and circumstances, they believed God and God commended them for their faith.

David, Hannah, the woman with the issue of blood and Martha of Bethany each came to the Lord. At some point each approached Christ in faith regarding their circumstances. David repented and reckoned with God by faith and walked in His ways. The woman with the issue of blood was healed after she approached and touched Christ in faith believing in the person and authority of Jesus. Martha submitted to Christ's counsel and continued to grow in faith. Hannah approached the throne of God to ask for a son and by faith, gave back to God the son she had not yet received. Hannah received a son from the Lord who became a prophet. God gave Hannah additional children. Likewise, when a Christian woman comes to the Lord earnestly in faith desiring to know and do His will, she can expect great things to happen. She can expect God's grace for restoration, direction, healing, and peace. God will meet our needs.

There is no better time to enhance and exercise faith than in the midst of a trial. Here are some practical ways we can exercise faith and hurdle stress:

- Make sure you are in a right standing with the Lord (1 John 1:9).
- Identify and read Scriptures that give hope and strength (1 Corinthians 10:13).
- Meditate and stand on the promises of God in faith (Isaiah 43:1–7).
- Make Christ the object of your faith. He is the master example and source of our faith (Hebrews 12:2).
- Purchase books, music and tapes that will strengthen your faith.
- Submit to the instructions God gives pertaining to your situation regardless of how you feel (James 4:7–10). Be patient with yourself, yet not negligent nor slothful.

- Transfer the principles of faith you use from an area in your life where we have strong faith and apply them to the present situation.
- Seek out help, when necessary, from your pastor, Christian counselor, or spiritually mature friend.
- Ward off Satan with Scripture when he floods your mind with the temptation to worry. Keep repeating God's truth to yourself and keep praying for yourself. Satan does not want us to know just how free we are.
- Meditate on and memorize Scripture.
- Enjoy some form of recreation and rest at the right time.
- Comfort yourself with God's love (Jeremiah 29:11; Romans 8:31, 35–39; 1 John 4:18).

The more confident we are of God's love, the less we will fear. The fact is, God loves us and there is nothing we will go through that He is not there. He is there to comfort, help, and guide us. All we need do is ask.

Faith is believing God is and a rewarder of those who diligently seek Him. Trust is accepting and relying on the character and heart of God. Dependence is waiting on the Lord to bring about what He has promised.

Hurdling Stress with Prayer

"The prayer of a righteous man is powerful and effective" (James 5:16b). Through her faith prayers, the

Christian woman can bring down kingdoms, exercise justice, receive God's promises, shut the mouths of lions, quench fiery flames, escape trouble, gain strength and wisdom to combat opposition, receive back wayward children, handle difficulties, and endure persecution. Scripture tells us that our struggle is not against flesh and blood, but against the rulers, authorities and powers and spiritual forces of evil in the heavenly realms (Ephesians 6:12).

Up to and beyond his last day in high school, my youngest son experienced injustice. My husband and I agreed that what he experienced in his last days should not go unchallenged. One week after he graduated, I met with the principal and outlined the occurrences of injustice our son suffered. Prayerfully, calmly, and diplomatically I presented the issues. All but one of the accusations were refuted. As I sat and listened to each rebuttal, I realized we were challenging an institution much bigger than ourselves. I left the office second-guessing the offenses suffered. As I continued to ponder the facts, I knew I had done the right thing and thereto left it in God's hands.

My husband and I did not share the incidents with anyone else in our community. Just a few months later, I was asked to serve on a committee that would grant me the opportunity to have a major voice amongst the school staff on behalf of the student.

In Acts 12, the church was under great persecution. John's brother, James was put to death. When Herod saw that this pleased the people, he arrested Peter. The

Bible says that the church prayed earnestly to God for him. God heard their prayers and sent His angels to supernaturally release Peter despite his chains.

When the church prayed, God answered. But let us look closely. Among the church were praying women. The prayer meeting was being held in Mary's house. When Peter knocked at the door, Rhoda, the servant answered it. Ladies, through the power of prayer we can overcome whatever comes our way and the way of our sisters in Christ. What kind of kingdom is threatening the doors of your life or family? Do you need courage to speak the truth in love or speak peace to a troubled situation? Are you faced with ridicule? Or persecution? Are you in need of mental, physical or emotional strength? Do you need wisdom for direction or decisions? Do you need divine intervention? "What other nation is so great as to have their gods near them the way the LORD our God is near us whenever we pray to him" (Deuteronomy 4:7).

HURDLING STRESS THROUGH WORSHIP

"And we rejoice in hope of the glory of God" (Romans 5:2b).

"Shadrach, Meshach and Abednego replied to the king, "O Nebuchadnezzar, we do not need to defend ourselves before you in this matter. If we are thrown into the blazing furnace, the God we serve is able to save us from it, and he will rescue us from your

hand, O king. But even if he does not, we want you to know, O king, that we will not serve your gods or worship the image of gold you have set up"(Daniel 3:16–18).

King Nebuchadnezzar leaped to his feet in amazement and asked his advisers, "Weren't there three men that we tied up and threw into the fire?" He said, "Look! I see four men walking around in the fire, unbound and unharmed, and the fourth looks like a son of the gods." Then Nebuchadnezzar said, "Praise be to the God of Shadrach, Meshach and Abednego, who has sent his angel and rescued his servants! They trusted in him and defied the king's command and were willing to give up their life rather than serve or worship any god except their own God. Therefore I decree that the people of any nation or language who say anything against the God of Shadrach, Meshach and Abednego be cut into pieces and their houses be turned into piles of rubble, for no other god can save in this way" (Daniel 3:24–25,28–29).

Our dear friend Job said, ". . . Naked I came from my mother's womb, and naked I will depart. The LORD gave and the LORD has taken away; may the name of the Lord be praised" (Job 1:21–22). The Bible says through all this, Job did not sin nor did he blame God. Praise and worship God no matter how you feel and no matter what you're going through. God is still God. Praise God for who He is, not just for what He can and will do for you. Praise Him because He has not ceased to be God, He has not abdicated His throne.

Hurdling Stress through Service

Do not stay where you are and drown yourself with your past or present situation. Resist the temptation to wallow in self-pity. But rather, set your heart and mind on the new; live in your new knowledge and deliverance. Those who bear spiritual fruit, God prunes that they might bear more fruit. For it is His will that we bear much fruit (John 15:2,8). We suffer affliction and are comforted by the Lord so that we in turn might comfort others with that same comfort. Our stones are turned into bread that others may eat and be satisfied (2 Corinthians 1:3–7). Lastly, Scriptures tell us that we have not a High Priest who cannot be touched with the feelings of our infirmities, but One who has been tempted in all things, yet without sin (Hebrews 4:15–16). Likewise, the trials you and I encounter bring about sensitivity in our hearts that equip us to minister to the heartfelt needs of others. Reach out to help others.

Whatever promise God gives you from His Word pertaining to your circumstances, BELIEVE! Be motivated, courageous, and steadfast in your faith. God blessed Noah's life and family because he believed God (Genesis 7:1, 8:1, 9:1). Enoch was taken up because he was a man known to believe and walk with God (Genesis 5:21–24). God gets excited when we take Him at His Word (Hebrews 11:6)! Don't be dissuaded or discouraged by persons or your circumstances in the midst of your trials. Whatever God has promised, stand on it and believe. He will bring it to pass (Hebrews 6:9–15). What you believe God has promised, must be in accordance to His Word. Faith is not claiming what we want. Faith is accepting and believing whatever the Bible says about our circumstances.

PRAYER

Dear Lord, I have been worried about my circumstances. I've spent my energy blaming others and my circumstances in order to relieve my anguish. What I realized is that my anxiety, as understandable as it may be, is a sign of my lack of faith in You. You love me and are in control. With just a word, You can deliver my family and me from these circumstances. Help me to glean what it is You want me to learn out of this situation. Lord, show me my personal and sinful contribution to the situation. I repent of my sin. Please cleanse me as I walk in Your ways.

Thank You for forgiveness and the grace to see this to the end. Lord, I worship You. Show me how to serve others and I will trust You to deliver my family and me. As You do, I will use what I have learned to help and pray for others who encounter similar circumstances. You said in all things give thanks. Lord, thank You for my trials, for through them You make me strong. Thank You for the grace and wisdom to live under unchanged circumstances. Thank You for deliverance.

Scenario, "Stressing the Point"

Doris comes to you, after 15 years of marriage and five children, and shares that she wants to leave home. She has been diagnosed with high blood pressure and is experiencing hives and pressure in her neck and head. She explains that her husband keeps blowing the budget and that they are up to their necks in debt. He doesn't lead and she is tired of filling in the gap on his behalf. The kids are messy, like their dad. Every time she tries to discipline the children, they say, "But Dad said." What words of hope would you give Doris?

CHAPTER 12

The Christian Woman's Influence

A voice of one calling in the desert, "Prepare the way for the Lord, make straight paths for Him" (Mark 1:3).

Voice is used for audible communication and can be identified as an instrument of sound that expresses opinion, choice or a wish. Its sound can also be used to communicate a distinction of form such as vowels and consonants or a system of inflections. Voice can also be characterized as influential power.

Throughout the history of Old Testament times, the 400 silent years or inter-testament times, New Testament times, time of the Early Church, and the present, women have influenced our society. What we say and do touches the lives of others. Our depth of influence reaches those around and beyond us. The quality of our influence is shaped by our response to God's purpose, plan, and design for us as we submit to Him (as light and salt - Matthew 5:13–16 and as a branch-John 15:1–11). To do otherwise, we risk becoming examples of women whose lives do not honor God, whose effect on society is damaging, and whose lives are destroyed. Let us take a closer look at a few examples of both godly and ungodly women of influence.

PERIOD: **OLD TESTAMENT**

WOMAN: Jezebel - Ungodly woman of influence
ACTS: Persecution and destruction of the prophets of the Lord (1 Kings 18:4,13).
    Persecution of the Prophet, Elijah (1 Kings 19:2).
    Conspiracy against Naboth, to spoil his vineyard (1 Kings 21:1–16).
    Evil Counsel to, and influence over her husband, Ahab (1 Kings 21:17–27; 2 Kings 9:30–37).
CONSEQUENCES: She died a horrible death, was thrown out of the window, eaten by dogs, and trampled upon by horses.

PERIOD: **OLD TESTAMENT**

WOMEN: Midwives - Godly women of influence
ACTS: They feared God and would not submit to the ungodly counsel of the Egyptian king.
    They let the Hebrew baby boys live (Exodus 1:15–21).

CONSEQUENCES: God was kind to them and gave them families of their own.

PERIOD: **400 SILENT YEARS - INTER TESTA- MENT TIMES (no revelation from God)**

WOMAN: CLEOPATRA - Ungodly woman of influence (An ancient Egyptian queen)
ACTS: Married brother (common) and he became co-ruler with her. She married 3 times. Cleopatra was a manipulator for power. She had her brother killed so she and Caesar's son could rule.[1]
CONSEQUENCES: Cleopatra committed suicide after failure to befriend Octavia, her husband's previous co-ruler and rival and for fear of humiliation.

PERIOD: **400 SILENT YEARS - INTER TESTA- MENT TIMES (no revelation from God)**

WOMEN: Jewish women revealed in old Jewish writings - Godly women of influence
ACTS: Typify the ideal womanly virtues of devout piety, ardent patriotism, poetic fervor and wifely devotion.[2]
CONSEQUENCES: Word of God moved on, John the Baptist parents, Zechariah and Elizabeth came out of that era, as well as Joseph and Mary the mother of Jesus, and Mary, the mother of Jesus found favor with God to carry the Christ child.

243

PERIOD: **NEW TESTAMENT TIMES**

WOMAN: Herodias, Herod's sister-in-law, and wife
- Ungodly woman of influence
ACTS: Used daughter to manipulate the beheading
of John the Baptist (Matthew 14:1–11; Mark
6:17–28).
CONSEQUENCES: Unknown (However, the Scriptures say "Do not to touch God's anointed and
do His servants no harm" (2 Chronicles 16:22;
Psalm 105:15).

PERIOD: **NEW TESTAMENT TIMES**

WOMAN: The Samaritan Woman - Godly woman
of influence
ACTS: Prior to salvation, she had many husbands
and her last was her live-in significant other.
Following salvation she shared her faith with
others (John 4:7–30; 39–42).
CONSEQUENCES: Many Samaritans placed their
faith in Christ through her witness.

PERIOD: **EARLY CHURCH**

WOMAN: Sapphira - Ungodly woman of influence
ACTS: Lied and schemed with her husband to keep
money previously committed to the church for
the work of God (Acts 5:1–11).
CONSEQUENCES: God took her life immediately.

PERIOD: **EARLY CHURCH**

WOMEN: Lois and Eunice - Godly women of influence
ACTS: Raised a godly grandson, and son (2 Timothy 1:2–5).
CONSEQUENCES: Timothy became a co-worker with Paul and was used greatly for the work of the ministry.

PERIOD: **PRESENT CHURCH AGE OF GRACE**

WOMAN: Madalyn Murray O'Hair - Ungodly woman of influence
ACTS: Fought against prayer in public schools and won.[3]
CONSEQUENCES: Moral deterioration, disruption, disorder and violence in our schools. A proliferation of moral decay that has given rise to rebellion and diffidence to Christian values in our nation. Madalyn Murray O'Hair's name is not recorded in the World Book Encyclopedia. Madalyn Murray O'Hair, along with one of her sons and granddaughter was deceived, robbed of their organization's financial resources, and murdered by her administrative assistant and his accomplice.

PERIOD: **PRESENT CHURCH AGE OF GRACE**

WOMAN: Sonya Carson - Godly woman of influence

ACTS: Raised two sons to believe God under economically and emotionally trying circumstances.

CONSEQUENCES: Both boys worked their way to the top of their class in junior high school.

Ben Carson, M.D. is a graduate of Yale University and the University of Michigan Medical School, and presently is the director of pediatric neurosurgery at Johns Hopkins University Hospital in Baltimore, Maryland.

Throughout the ages, we consistently see women exercising their voice to persuade others for good or evil, giving life or death. This practice is more commonly known as the power of influence, and is a unique ability, I believe, given to women when God fashioned and ordained woman as a helpmate (Genesis 2:18).

Each of these aforementioned women utilized their position to promote either their personal cause or the cause of God. We need never be ashamed of our position—whether we are a housewife, a stay-at-home mom or a major player in the boardroom of a conglomerate organization; whether we are surviving on limited financial means or financially prosperous. Regardless of where we stand, we carry the unique ability to make a difference in the lives of our family, church and community.

Christian women who trust God with their dreams and disappointments, who walk daily in obedience to the revealed will of God, and who use their present position to honor Him, are women of divine purpose and influence. They impact the world around them with God. This is evident in the lives of the Hebrew mid-wives of the Old Testament, the Jewish women of inter-testament times, the Samaritan woman of the New Testament, Lois and Eunice of the early church. Dr. Ben Carson, son of Sonya Carson has said, "It would be impossible to tell about my accomplishments without starting with my mother's influence."[4]

FORMS OF COMMUNICATION

Let us look at seven forms of communication we use daily. We may not be aware of their potential effects or ministry, but when a Christian woman places them under the direction of Scripture and the guidance of the Holy Spirit, the results are phenomenal.

Speech

Women have never been at a loss for words. Our sister Eve cashed in on her need to speak to the devil regarding eating from the tree of knowledge of good and evil. Sarah communicated her point to Abraham about how she felt he needed to give God a hand in the promise for an offspring. We would be remiss if we failed to acknowledge Miriam who felt it her personal responsibility to instruct Moses on how to lead God's people, and whom he should marry. Michal sarcastically criticized David when he danced before the LORD in celebration of the homecoming of the Ark of the Covenant to the city of David. Then there was Job's wife who felt a need to counsel Job, in renouncing the one and only hope he had—his God.

A Christian woman must govern her speech. "A word aptly spoken is like apples of gold in settings of silver" (Proverbs 25:11).

STOP to think and pray before you speak. Be considerate. Use your voice to speak the truth in love. Be cautious not to call a right, wrong nor a wrong, right (Ephesians 4:15, 6:14). Share the gospel with the unsaved (Acts 1:8). Teach and share with single women how to live pure lives (1 Thessalonians 4:3–8) and to serve the Lord (1 Corinthians 7:34). Walk with and gingerly admonish young married women to love and respect their husbands and to love their children (Ephesians 5:22–24,33; Titus 2:4–5). Encourage and edify the saints (Romans 15:1–4). Turn from foolish conversation, arguing or slander of any kind.

Making sport of the weaknesses of our husband and/or children and comparing our strengths and weaknesses with those of other women is not acceptable nor becoming for a Christian woman. God may show us a weakness in another person's life. More often than not, the reason God has shown us is that we might join Him and pray for them. It is not always God's will that we give our verbal opinion. Allow God to transform your opinion into a genuine prayer of concern and service. Finally, we must avoid at all costs criticizing others externally and in our hearts. Being critical destroys love, damages another's self-worth and mars our coun-tenance and faith.

"We all stumble in many ways. If anyone is never at fault in what he says, he is a perfect man, able to keep his whole body in check" (James 3:2).

"When words are many, sin is not absent, but he who holds his tongue is wise" (Proverbs 10:19).

"A time to be silent and a time to speak" (Ecclesi-astes 3:7b).

The Bible testifies, "For out of the overflow of the heart the mouth speaks. The good man brings good things out of the good stored up in him, and the evil man brings evil things out of the evil stored up in him" (Matthew 12:34b–35).

Heart

A Christian woman must govern her heart. "Above all else, guard your heart, for it is the wellspring of life" (Proverbs 4:23).

Being a positive and effective influence begins with a pure heart. "The Lord saw how great man's wickedness on the earth had become, and that every inclination of the thoughts of his heart was only evil all the time. The Lord was grieved that he had made man on the earth, and his heart was filled with pain" (Genesis 6:5–6).

A pure heart is a changed heart. "And by that will, we have been made holy through the sacrifice of the body of Jesus Christ once for all" (Hebrews 10:10). As adopted daughters of God through the death and resurrection of our Lord and Savior, Jesus Christ, we have been made holy (Ephesians 1:4–8). Now, we must live holy lives. "As obedient children, do not conform to the evil desires you had when you lived in ignorance. But just as he who called you is holy, so be holy in all you do; for it is written: 'Be holy, because I am holy'" (1 Peter 1:14–16).

Keep a clean heart by immediately acknowledging and confessing sin to God (1 John 1:9; Psalm 51). Initiate reconciliation in any broken relationships (Matthew 5:23–26; Matthew 18:15–17). Exercise forgiveness promptly (Matthew 18:21–22,35). Conduct a regular intake of Scripture (Psalm 119:11). Have no union or bonds with an unbeliever (2 Corinthians 6:14–18). Have no association with an angry person (Proverbs 22:24–25).

Finally, be willing to examine the motivation of your heart. The phrase, "To thing own self be true" by William Shakespeare captures the essence of this principle. Stop. Examine your motives and be honest with yourself. God already knows. Be willing to admit the truth about you to yourself. "He who conceals his sins does not prosper, but whoever confesses and renounces them finds mercy" (Proverbs 28:13). Confront your motives with the truth of Scripture and keep the room of your heart swept clean from sin.

"A heart at peace gives life to the body, but envy rots the bones" (Proverbs 14:30).

Conduct (Behavior)

A Christian woman must govern her conduct. "Likewise teach older women to be reverent in the way they live, not to be slanderers or addicted to much wine" (Titus 2:3).

Be sure to conduct yourself in a manner appropriate for one living in the presence of the Lord. Fear the Lord (Psalm 111:10). Examine whether everything you do can stand up to the test of doing it in the name of the Lord (Colossians 3:17). Show respect for your neighbor (Romans 13:9–10); strive to control your emotions and maintain your composure (Titus 2:12–14).

"When a man's ways are pleasing to the LORD, he makes even his enemies live at peace with him" (Proverbs 16:7).

Choices (decisions)

A Christian woman must govern her choices. "Your word is a lamp to my feet and a light for my path" (Psalm 119:105).

Strive to maintain innocence in your private life as well as your public life (Philippians 2:12). God's desire is for truth to reside within the depths of our inner being (Proverbs 10:9,16; Psalm 51:6). Seek wise counsel (Proverbs 15:22); stay focused and keep your feet from evil (Proverbs 4:25–27).

"The path of the righteous is like the first gleam of dawn, shining ever brighter till the full light of day" (Proverbs 4:18).

"Gray hair is a crown of splendor; it is attained by a righteous life" (Proverbs 16:31).

Natural Talent and Spiritual Gifts

A Christian woman must use her natural abilities and spiritual gifts. "For God's gifts and his call are irrevocable" (Romans 11:29).

Serve God (Exodus 31:1–11; Mark 15:41; 1 Corinthians 15:58) and be your best for Him (Deuteronomy 11:13; Joshua 22:5; 1 Samuel 12:24). Assist in the well-being of others (Luke 8:2–3 and 1 Peter 4:10) and use your abilities as a resource (Proverbs 31:18).

"A generous man will prosper; he who refreshes others will himself be refreshed" (Proverbs 11:25).

"I have given skill to all the craftsmen to make everything I have commanded you" (Exodus 31:6).

"To these four young men God gave knowledge and understanding of all kinds of literature and learning. And Daniel could understand visions and dreams of all kinds" (Daniel 1:17).

Prayer

A Christian woman must be a woman of prayer. "And when he had taken it, the four living creatures and the twenty-four elders fell down before the Lamb. Each one had a harp and they were holding golden bowls full of incense, which are the prayers of the saints" (Revelation 5:8).

Spending time talking with God helps us get to know Him and our own personal limits (Romans 8:26). Learn to rely on God's perspective and commit your mind, heart, and will to trust in the promises and power of God more than the faithfulness of men (Hebrews 11:6).

"For the eyes of the Lord are on the righteous and his ears are attentive to their prayer, but the face of the Lord is against those who do evil" (1 Peter 3:12).

"If you believe, you will receive whatever you ask for in prayer" (Matthew 21:22).

Spirit

A Christian woman must govern her spirit. The need to control one's spirit requires time and attention. One needs time to think, meditate, and exercise various forms of mental rest and relaxation. One way to attain a managed spirit is by taking the time to meditate on a passage of Scripture. Work the passage through your mind by asking what it says, what it means, and how it applies to your life. Throughout the day, bring the passage up again for reprocessing. Meditation does not have to be strenuous. Simply lying across your bed or leaning back in a comfortable chair will suffice. Close your eyes and pray for understanding taking the passage of Scripture a little at a time. You will walk away renewed and rejoicing. You may even slip into a peaceful sleep.

A good time for Scripture meditation is on your lunch break or before bed (Joshua 1:8; Psalm 1:2).

Mental relaxation exercises may include a good workout followed by a warm shower, reading Scripture or a good book with a cup of herbal tea, listening to a musical recording of nature, watching a comedy, taking a candle-light bath with scented bath crystals, a warm shower, or sleep.

Take some time to thoroughly think through your goals, decisions, problems, ideas, and advice (to be given to others or received). Ask God for wisdom, be willing to listen for God and avoid being in a hurry to draw conclusions regarding any of the above matters. After you talk out and think through various scenarios write them down for visual observation. A good way to think is to go for a long walk, talking to God as you go and letting Him talk back to you. Share your ideas with Him. He will respond. You will return home relaxed, refreshed and most of the time with a solution.

As a follower of Christ, work hard to maintain your composure both internally and externally, under all circumstances. Silence is as necessary as speaking. Keeping silent, taking a walk, and praying can change our perspective on a situation. Taking two minutes to refrain from speaking or reacting and adding a teaspoon of positive thought or humor gives the air a chance to cool.

"In your anger do not sin; when you are on your beds, search your hearts and be silent" (Psalm 4:4).

"He that is slow to anger is better than the mighty; and he that ruleth his spirit than he that taketh a city" (Proverbs 16:32 KJV).

"A man of understanding is even-tempered" (Proverbs 17:27b).

In all of the areas of communication mentioned above, none are effective apart from love. What we say becomes positively ineffective if it is not coupled with love. Regardless of who we are and what we possess, without love, the Bible says it amounts to nothing. The magnitude and value of what we do and gain is determined by the presence of love. Our Christian witness and testimony is ineffective regardless of our position and authority if we do not have love (1 Corinthians 13:1–3).

Being women of divine purpose and influence—making a difference by impacting the world around us with God—involves having the heart and mind of Christ, who became a servant for our encouragement and hope. As we move out, let us be reminded to bear with the failings of the weak and not please self. "Each of us should please his neighbor for his good, to build him up" (Romans 15:1–2). The Christian woman makes a difference because she is DIFFERENT!

AREAS OF INFLUENCE

- What are the responsibilities and needs of your home (family and house)?

- What support does your husband need (emotional, financial or prayer)?
- What are the needs in your church?
- What are the needs in your community? Do you know your city and state officials? Are you a registered voter? Do you support or utilize elected officials?

I have shared throughout this book that I am a housewife, a stay-at-home mom and a homeschool educator. As easy-going as it may appear to some, these roles have difficulties like everything else. At one time I did not get out on my own much nor did I have as many opportunities to interact with people on a regular basis. The following are just a few examples of how God has used the scope of my world for His glory. I am sharing them as a means of encouraging you to believe that God will make a difference right where you are as you submit to Him. Our stories may be similar or they may vary, but what is important is that as Christian women, we recognize that God will use us right where we are to impact the world around us. He uses our speech, hearts, conduct, natural talent and abilities, prayer and a controlled spirit as we submit to Him.

While shopping with my husband one day, I initiated conversation with the saleslady who was fitting him. As we engaged in conversation, a customer who needed help interrupted us. So I began to pray for God's guidance and intervention. We resumed our discussion and as the salesperson proceeded to close out the purchase, another customer came along. I noticed that the salesperson wanted to talk further so I asked the Lord to send the customer away. The sales lady, unaware of my prayer, then telephoned for help for the waiting customer.

As I shared Christ with the saleslady, she said, "I watched you as you entered the floor and I said to myself, there is something different about that woman. She walks with a sense of peace and ease like no one I've ever known." At once I was eager to share (she struggled with unforgiveness) that it was Jesus and He could likewise give her the power to forgive those (professed Christians) who had mistreated her. She wanted to know more. We exchanged telephone numbers to meet for lunch.

A friend of mine, whose career had become stagnant, came to me with her frustration. We looked in the Bible to see what God wanted to do in her life if only she would let go and give the control back to God. She went home and committed herself to doing it God's way. In less than one year, her career exploded beyond her imagination, both nationally and internationally.

Each morning during the week, my children and I would stand at the bus stop talking and praying before they went off to school (my daughter was in school outside the home at the time). We lived across the street from the high school my sons attended. At that time of day many cars would come by. One morning a lady stopped her car, rolled down her window and said, "I watch you every morning and I wanted you to know, you are a blessing to me. You are what a good family looks like." As she drove away, my heart was encouraged.

My daughter's class was assigned to read a book that my husband and I felt was laced with satanic imagery. We wrote a letter to her teacher outlining our personal and spiritual convictions from the Bible. One week passed when we were informed that Jennifer would not have to read the book along with her class. She could sit in the office and read a book of our choosing.

We play tennis as a family sport. One summer, my youngest son, who was sixteen at the time, my daughter who was eight at the time and I, played tennis together, daily. There were groups of women there who played doubles together. One day they asked if I would like to play with them at which time they expressed how impressed they were that my teenager didn't mind playing with me. They also commented on how well the two children played together. In the weeks that followed, the women began bringing their children to play with them and my children.

One of my sons was not heeding the advice of my husband and me. I was concerned for his life. I prayed and asked God to speak to him and that my son would clearly hear Him. No more than two minutes after getting off my knees, I received a telephone call from my son saying he had just been in a car accident. He explained that he was okay. He just injured his lip, but the car was damaged. God spoke to our son giving him the same words we had given him. He heard and heeded God's voice with a made up mind to live God's way. By the way, the car was totaled, but God kept my son.

*But thanks be to God, who always leads us in trium-
phal procession in Christ and through us spreads
everywhere the fragrance of the knowledge of him.
For we are to God the aroma of Christ among those
who are being saved and those who are perishing.
To the one we are the smell of death; to the other, the
fragrance of life. And who is equal to such a task?
Unlike so many, we do not peddle the word of God
for profit. On the contrary, in Christ we speak before God with sincerity, like men sent from God (2
Corinthians 2:14–17).*

MAY THE FOOTPRINTS YOU
LEAVE BEHIND MATCH
THOSE WHO RESIDE
IN YOU

PRAYER

Dear Lord, each step has been a difficult one as Your
Word confronted the real me. I've come too far to turn
back now. So here I am at the altar again asking You to
please forgive me for not taking personal responsibility
for how I have utilized my voice (speech, heart, conduct, choices, talents, spiritual gifts, prayer, my spirit,
and Your love). I want my hands, mouth, heart and
my mind to be used to glorify You and edify my family,
friends and neighbors, even my enemies. I am committing to being cognizant of how I use my voice. Please
sensitize my spirit to do Your will and quicken me when

I am approaching sin in this area. Make me a woman of divine purpose and influence for Your glory.

SCENARIO, "LEGAL HELP"

Your excitement over the new para-legal job you worked hard and asked the Lord for has diminished to a dimly lit wick. You have worked with your boss for nearly one month and have already reached high levels of frustration. Your boss is impatient, demanding and belligerent. What will you do?

CHAPTER 13

The Christian Woman's Journey

PURPOSE FOR THE JOURNEY

The duty of every man is to fear God and keep His commandments (Ecclesiastes 12:13). The Christian woman's goal as she journeys through life is to live to please the Lord. We keep God, His will, and purposes before us through reading and the studying of His Word. "I don't have time" is a fallacy. For the Christian woman and all she is responsible for, there is nothing and no one more important than spending time with God in the Word and prayer - not her job, her mate, her children, nor the urgent things of the day. We have to develop a system for learning God's Word, accepting God's Word into our heart, and in faith, making daily application of the principles we learn. As we journey through the seasons of our life, God's Word will grow us toward spiritual maturity and intimacy as we surrender to Him. Simply and quietly, make room in your life for God. In the end, you will not be disappointed. You will experience what is His good, pleasing, and perfect will for you (Romans 12:1–2).

Our purpose is to live to please the Lord and to be like Him. In Matthew 20:28, Jesus said that He came not to be served, but rather to serve and give His life as a ransom for many. One of the attributes that links us with Christ is having a servant's heart. Unfortunately, we live in a self-centered and self-driven society, where the focus is on "me." That attitude has made its way into Christian psychology and the Christian church. We have lost words such as sacrifice, commitment, devotion, and self-denial from our vocabulary and life style. The focus is now on how God will minister to *me* and meet *my* deepest innermost need. We have lost sight of our mission to serve Jesus Christ. The Christian community has become emotionally needy and it is rendering us inoperative.

Throughout the book it was my goal to articulate God's revealed will for the Christian woman and to provide the necessary tools for good personal and home management, while providing a voice that identified, addressed and gave comfort to the needs of the reader. While the Christian woman does have a need to be ministered to as she ministers to the needs of so many, we must keep in mind why we are here and who we are serving. Yes, the Christian woman who takes her role and responsibilities seriously, does get tired, feels forgotten and unappreciated and feels like there is no end to her giving. But if we flip that canvas over, like we will see Paul do later in this chapter, what we see are the qualities of Christian character such as sacrifice, devotion, commitment, and self-denial, which all spell love. Yes, there is a balance which we learned and strive to practice. But, the world and its philosophies must not fool us. We are to follow Jesus Christ and work hard to be like Him. Christ gave his all; He gave his life. Let us give our lives to serve Jesus Christ in every area of our lives. What we do for our family, on our job, in our church and community is neither for our fame and glory nor to please man, but to please our Lord and Savior, Jesus Christ.

A PLAN FOR THE JOURNEY

Do not fret because of evil men or be envious of those who do wrong; for like the grass they will soon wither, like green plants they will soon die away. Trust in the LORD and do good; dwell in the land and enjoy safe pasture. Delight yourself in the LORD and he will give you the desires of your heart. Commit your way to the LORD; trust in him and he will do this: He will make your righteousness shine like the dawn, the justice of your cause like the noonday sun. Be still before the LORD and wait patiently for him; do not fret when men succeed in their ways, when they carry out their wicked schemes. Refrain from anger and turn from wrath; do not fret-it leads only to evil.

For evil men will be cut off, but those who hope in the LORD will inherit the land (Psalm 37:1–9).

POWER FOR THE JOURNEY

How do we accomplish all that is required of us in Scripture? The standard is high. We need more than our natural mind and skill to carry it out. We need wisdom, strength, encouragement, and hope. God has given us the Holy Spirit to do just that and more. The Holy Spirit is the third person in the Trinity. The Holy Spirit is a person. The Holy Spirit is God. The moment you and I were saved, we were permanently indwelled by God the Holy Spirit.

The Holy Spirit will never leave us (John 14:16). The role of the Holy Spirit is to empower the believer (Acts 1:8), to help, prompt, convict us of sin, to guide, teach and illuminate the mind. We are told in Scripture to be filled with the Spirit (Ephesians 5:18). Just like filling the gas tank of a car with gasoline, so we are filled with God, the Holy Spirit. We can't see the gas as it goes in nor as it escapes. We can't feel the gas as we ride in our cars, but we know it is in there because we put it there. Also the gas gauge tells us it is there and when we pull off, the car moves on to its destination on a power it could not without the gas. Likewise, we accept the filling of God the Holy Spirit by faith, not according to our feelings, but on the basis that He said He would fill us. As we rely on Him, we are able to do what we could not on our own. Listen to see if this passage explains why you and I may not feel anything: "The wind blows wherever it pleases. You hear its sound, but you cannot tell where it comes from or where it is going. So it is with everyone born of the Spirit" (John 3:8).

Although the Holy Spirit never leaves us, two things can hinder His work and power in the believer's life. A Christian woman can quench the Spirit by NOT doing or saying what the Spirit prompts her to (1 Thessalonians 5:19). She can grieve the Spirit by sinning against God (Ephesians 4:30). The former is the sin of omission and the latter, the sin of commission. In either instance, the way to be filled again is by confessing sin to God and asking for forgiveness. God is faithful and just to forgive and cleanse us from all our unrighteousness (1 John 1:9; 2:1–2). Instantly, we are forgiven and filled with the Holy Spirit. We may not necessarily feel like it, but when we move out in faith and the trustworthiness of God and His Word we will find it to be true.

Because we live (alive spiritually) by the Spirit (John 3:3–8; Galatians 2:20), we are told that we should also walk by the Spirit (Galatians 5:25). Two ways a Christian woman can be assured of walking by the Spirit is to remain filled by confessing all known sin and submitting to the Word of God (John 15:5,7–8). The importance of submitting to the Word of God is that God's Word is alive. It has the power to regenerate and transform. It will teach us what to do and how.

Just as our cars depend on gas to run, so we must depend on God the Holy Spirit to live the Christian life. Evidence of walking by the Spirit will be seen by our love, joy, peace, patience, kindness, goodness, faithful-ness, gentleness, and self-control (Galatians 5:22–23). This is where many of us get stuck. We work hard trying to produce these traits ourselves.

I remember reading Galatians 5:22–23 years ago and wondering is this something I do? Will Christ do it or both? I went to a friend to inquire and she gave me no answer. I came to learn that it is the Spirit's fruit (production), the very character and nature of Christ (Matthew 11:28 and 1 Peter 3:4). The Spirit will pro-duce His character in us, but we have to submit to His inner working. By confessing all known sin and abiding in Christ and His Word abiding in us, we can hear, see, and submit to the inner working of the Holy Spirit. To live holy and righteous, we must live under the Holy Spirit's control.

We have to die so that Christ can live His life through us. Giving God control of our mind, heart, and will does not mean we lose our freedom or stop thinking. It simply means we choose to yield our mind, heart, and will to the Word of God.

When the Scriptures says to walk, it means to go through our daily routine staying in touch with God through prayer: "Lord, how should I respond?" The Holy Spirit will lead the Christian woman by illumi-nating her mind with the Word of God. Then we are responsible for obeying or carrying it out. If we do not hear anything different from what we have chosen to do (presupposing we have prayed and live according the Scriptures to the best of our knowledge), we can follow through. The Holy Spirit will let us know when a change is in order.

We cannot obey the Word of God unless we are in fellowship with God. It is the Spirit of God that gives us wisdom, and the power to carry out His will. Is there anything we do? Yes. Pray on all occasions, stay in fellowship with God by confessing all known sin, read God's Word on a regular basis, submit to the Word of God, and submit to the Holy Spirit's leading.

If we do not experience the presence and control of the Holy Spirit, perhaps there is sin in our life that we are not willing to let go of or some area in our life that we are not willing to turn over to God. Perhaps the problem is that we fight with God over His will for us as outlined in His Word. We fight His working in our daily life when we pout, complain, rebel, and envy our neighbor—all of which are deeds of our flesh (Galatians 5:19–21). Our attitude must be, "What is God's will for me?" Then when we know it, accept it and do it.

If we walk by the Spirit in obedience and discipline we will not carry out the desire of our flesh (the natural man). Walking according to the guidance of the Holy Spirit and the Word of God can be such a way of life that there is no room for the flesh to control. We always have a choice as to whether we will submit to God (our new nature) or our flesh (our old sin nature). When we submit to God, we do not allow our flesh to rule. When we submit to our flesh, we do not allow God to rule. Submitting to God gives life while submitting to the sin nature brings death. Walking by the Spirit is like a person who is dependent upon oxygen to provide air to his lungs to live and breathe. Likewise, a person who is controlled and walks by the Holy Spirit is dependent upon Him to speak, act and to ultimately please God.

For our Monday night Bible time, my children and I had been studying the rapture, the tribulation period, and the second coming of Jesus. In doing so, I was convicted that Christians tend not to tell people Jesus is coming back with the same passion that Noah used when he built the ark and warned the people of the impending rain. As a result, I made a solemn vow to tell people whose path I cross, that Jesus is coming very soon and to ask them whether or not they are ready.

One day, my washing machine broke. Not knowing exactly how to handle the situation, I felt my best option was to have devotional time with the Lord, praying for direction and favor in the situation. I called a repairman who could not come for two days. In the meantime, the thought came, "You said you would tell people Jesus was coming soon." I began to realize that God had a plan more pertinent than mine. At the time, my husband was due to leave for a week-long trip out of the country and there were items I still needed to wash and pack by 3:00 P.M.

God gave me the wisdom (the Laundromat) to get my husband's clothes washed and packed. I was able to lovingly send him on his way. The repairman arrived two days later as scheduled. While writing the check to pay him, I was reminded that I needed to tell him that Jesus is coming back and to ask him if he will be ready. He felt he could get to heaven by being good. I was able to share the plan of salvation with him and tell him how he could be assured that he was ready for Christ's return. God had a plan that differed from my own; I had to stay in step with God.

The standards God requires of Christian women are high. As Christian women, we have the tasks of living holy lives; being a godly single; lovingly submitting to our husband; teaching, training, nurturing and disciplining our children; keeping up the home; and possibly winning an unsaved mate to the Lord. We cannot achieve these endeavors apart from the help of the Holy Spirit. None of this is possible in our own strength over any length of time without resulting in frustration and the resolve to give up and quit. Even when we perform at our best, with the most earnest motivation, we are still limited. We need God's indwelling Holy Spirit for guidance and power.

GRACE FOR THE JOURNEY

There is one more thing I need to share if our lives and the lives of those around us are to be blessed. I had originally ended this chapter with living by the power Holy Spirit when God reminded me that there is yet another principle that has made a tremendous difference in my life—the blessing of living by God's grace. How can I tell you that it is God's grace that has truly liberated me and made all of the difference?

Sometimes there comes a point in our lives when it seems we can't go on. Nothing is externally wrong or out of place. We just find that we do not have the where-withal to go another step. We earnestly desire to listen and help others, but to no avail. We find that we have become emotionally tired. We attend church worship faithfully and perhaps even Bible study, but spiritu-ally, we are numb or blank. We get up in the morning ready to mentally tackle our day, but after five minutes, our body wants to return to bed. Physically we have become exhausted beyond what a day off or weekend can restore. We set out to make our to do list, but our thoughts are blurred. Attempts to pull the recesses of our mind together are not working. Mentally we notice that we are a bit slower than usual. After seeing the doctor, we are pleased to learn that there nothing medi-cally wrong. After working and pressing hard to meet everyone's needs for so long, we have lost our zeal. We have run out of steam. There is no going on and to do so would be harmful.

I have come to share that there is hope. There is a better way and brighter days ahead. Consider this passage:

Do you not know? Have you not heard? The LORD is the everlasting God, the Creator of the ends of the earth. He will not grow tired or weary, and his understanding no one can fathom. He gives strength to the weary and increases the power of the weak. Even youths grow tired and weary, and young men stumble and fall; but those who hope in the LORD will renew their strength. They will soar on wings like eagles; they will run and not grow weary, they will walk and not be faint" (Isaiah 40:28–31).

The first thing you should know is that you are not alone. God is with you. "Keep your lives free from the love of money and be content with what you have, because God has said, 'Never will I leave you; never will I forsake you'" (Hebrews 13:5). All we have to do is to call upon Him for help. "Let us then approach the throne of grace with confidence, so that we may receive mercy and find grace to help us in our time of need" (Hebrews 4:16). God never intended for man to live independent of Him.

Living our life is not incumbent upon us alone. We are responsible for living holy and righteous. However, when we've done all we know to do, we must rely on God's grace to do what we cannot and to make right what we do.

When my boys were young and learning how to make their beds, I would go in behind them and tuck a little here and straighten a little there giving the beds the finishing touches they needed. As they got older and their schoolwork became more demanding, to take the load off, my husband and I washed the dinner dishes or put out the trash for them. When the mental and time restraints became sometimes overwhelming for them, we pitched in to help them do what they could not. There were times we super-sized their fast food meals, took them out to dinner, or bought them their favorite snack or clothing item we knew they wanted just because we loved them and wanted to bless them. That is how it is with God's grace.

God's grace is an unmerited act or deed, an unmerited favor bestowed, an unmerited kindness or benefit. More specifically, it is His divine, unmerited favor, grace, benefit, blessing, and gift bestowed on us. "From the fullness of his grace we have all received one blessing after another" (John 1:16). Our salvation is the gracious and loving act of God through Christ. "For it is by grace you have been saved, through faith-and this not from yourselves, it is the gift of God-not by works, so that no one can boast" (Ephesians 2:8–9). When we placed our trust in Jesus and what He did on our behalf, the gracious favor and benefit bestowed on us was salvation with all of its ramifications. The wonderful thing about God's grace is that it does not stop at the door of our salvation.

God's grace *in you* will enable you to do great things (Acts 6:8). My husband had just completed his studies for his Master's degree. He maintained his role and responsibilities as a dedicated husband and faithful father. He discipled our oldest son who was away at school by speaking to him weekly and in some cases, daily. He continued the discipleship process with our younger son who was a senior in high school at the time and safely tucked our daughter to bed nightly. He traveled nationally and internationally for his job, oversaw a ministry and conducted counseling. Also during this time, his father went home to be with the Lord. He still managed to graduate with high academic honors. Personally, I don't know how he did it. Before he started out on this venture, he told the children and me "It won't be by power or might, but by God's Spirit" (Zechariah 4:6). And God's Spirit it was.

God has given His grace to us to render us useful for service in His kingdom (1 Corinthians 15:10; Ephesians 4:7). My father is an older man who frequents a nursing home to pray with the patients. There are several things that impress me about this. Over 10 years ago my dad was in a severe car accident that caused permanent injury. He received a hip replacement, but due to complications, it was removed and replaced by another one. That one was removed, but no replacement was given due to the risks involved. As a result, one of his legs is shorter than the other, which is compensated for by a lift on his shoe and by the assistance of a cane.

The nursing home my dad visits has six floors. He voluntarily visits the nursing home daily as the Lord gives him strength, covering 2 to 3 floors a day until he has seen all the patients. My father does not have a car; therefore, he catches public transportation. If there is an important family gathering or we are concerned about his rest his reply is, "When God says if you do it for the least . . . well . . . these are God's least and they have to know that God loves and cares about them." What I love is that he just doesn't pray for the patients, he listens to their concerns, encourages them with a touch or a hug and will wipe their tears from their eyes.

By God's grace, the Spirit of life has entered that nursing home. Patients who would not talk, now talk and sing. Patients who had given up and would not walk, now walk. Some of the workers have come into a personal relationship with God and are set on the road to a blessed life as a result of God's grace in my dad's life and his witness.

God's grace will be with you as it was with Moses . . . (Romans 16:20; Galatians 6:18; 2 John 3; 1 Thessalonians 5:28)

> . . . when his mother could no longer hide him, then placed him in a basket and sent him off down the Nile placing him in God's care (Exodus 2:3–4),
> . . . for his care after being found by Pharaoh's daughter (Exodus 2:5–10),
> . . . when he escaped and was protected from the Pharaoh's evil edict (Exodus 1:15,16,22; 2:2),
> . . . as he stood on God's Holy Mountain before the burning bush (Exodus 3:1–5),
> . . . as he stood before Pharaoh telling him to let God's people go (Exodus 5:1–4,22–23; 6:1),
> . . . when he brought the children of Israel out of Egypt (14:15–22),
> . . . when he received wisdom from his father-in-law, Jethro, as to how to lead the Hebrews (18:13–24),
> . . . when he received the Ten Commandments a second time (Exodus 34:1–2,27–29),
> . . . when God passed over him (Exodus 33:12–23),
> . . . when Israel defeated the Amalekites in battle (Exodus 17:8–16),

. . . as he looked over to see the promise land of Canaan (Deuteronomy 48–52),

God's grace will be upon you (Luke 2:40; Acts 4:33). God's grace was upon Jesus and the Apostles to do His will. God's grace will give you power, strength and wisdom to do what He has called you to. When I was the assistant director of our women's discipleship ministry, as issues arose, God would sometimes give me the answer right on the spot. There were other times He would give me the answers over the course of time. This was true even while parenting my children. There were times I did not know what to do. When God gave me the answer, sometimes I was too timid to carry it out. He gave me strength and reminded me not to look at their faces.

God's grace for you will render you strong (2 Corinthians 12:9). As the end drew near, I did not have the strength to complete this manuscript. The summer prior to the end began with my husband's travels, my older son landing in the hospital, and my younger son graduating. I was in a car accident, taking my final exams, and closing out my daughter's homeschool year. Within weeks my oldest son had a bad reaction to some medication which sent him into a deep depression for which my husband and I had to spend extensive hours counseling him through. There were trips to and from New York where our oldest son interned. I also traveled to Virginia to take care of my sister who had had surgery, during which time I also had a tape series evaluation to conduct.

By summer's end, my husband and I were exhausted. He was finishing up his requirements for school. The day he finished, we headed off to Atlanta to take both sons to school. In the process I met with my editor. After we dropped off our sons, we headed for a two-day get-away for rest and relaxation. The second day I was badly stung by men-of-war jellyfish. Upon our arrival home, school for my daughter had begun, and for me, was due to begin. I also needed to make revisions and additions to the manuscript. Two days before school was to start, I had a reaction from the sting of the jelly fish followed by back spasms that landed me in bed. The following week, my husband was out of town. The next week as I approached the manuscript once again, I came down with a terrible cold that again, you guessed it, landed me in bed.

The week that my husband was away however, there was a week long Spiritual Life Conference held at my church. The speaker's topic was perseverance. On the last night, all I could do was groan to the Lord in my spirit how tired I had become. The speaker's lesson that night taught us to lift our hands and arms up to the Lord in praise. And when we do, God will give us our second wind just as we receive air into our lungs when we lift our arms up over our heads. When I did, God gave me the strength and mental fortitude to persevere and see it through.

God's grace for you will make you a winner (Romans 5:17). Following Paul's conversion, he became a "slave" for the Lord and shared the perils of his Christian journey in great detail in 2 Corinthians 11:23, "I have worked much harder, been in prison more frequently, been flogged more severely, and been exposed to death again and again." In 2 Timothy 3:11, he conveys that the Lord rescued him from all of them. It is believed that even his death was a brutal one. Let us examine Paul's perspective:

> *For I am already being poured out like a drink of-fering, and the time has come for my departure. I have fought the good fight. I have finished the race, I have kept the faith. Now there is in store for me the crown of righteousness, which the Lord, the righteous Judge, will award to me on that day-and not only to me, but also to all who have longed for his appearing (2 Timothy 4:7–8).*

God's grace is greater than all our needs. In 1 Timothy 2:1, Paul charged Timothy to be strong in the grace that is in Christ Jesus. The strength Paul was speaking of was not his own but the supernatural strength which comes from the Lord. If we were to return to our original text in Isaiah 40, we learn that the LORD renews the strength of those who hope in Him. For He is everlasting (He doesn't get tired), the Creator of the ends of the earth (He has all power), and no one can fathom His understanding (He is all-wise) (Isaiah 40:28). Whether it is the strength to endure or handle something difficult

(Philippians 4:13), power (Ephesians 6:10; 2 Timothy 2:1), or a skill (Acts 9:22; 1 Timothy 1:12), God will renew our strength. Paul did not tell Timothy just to be strong, but strong in the grace of the Lord. When we learn to factor in and rely on God's grace, we will not just fly, but soar like an eagle, run and not get weary and walk and not faint. How? By the grace (goodness) of God. Then we can say like David, "Surely goodness and love will follow me all the days of my life, and I will dwell in the house of the LORD forever" (Psalm 23:6). Recognizing the goodness of God—His grace in your life will make a difference.

A Prayer for the Journey

May the God of peace, who through the blood of the eternal covenant brought back from the dead our Lord Jesus, that great Shepherd of the sheep, equip you with everything good for doing His will, and may he work in us what is pleasing to Him, through Jesus Christ, to whom be glory forever and ever (Hebrews 13:20–21).

Scenario, "She Did It Her Way"

Your elderly aunt, Aunt Mary, lives in Kentucky. Aunt Mary has no children and lives alone. You make a few yearly visits to make sure she is doing well. Following one visit, you notice that Aunt Mary is washing her clothing in the tub with a wash board. When you question her, she reasons that since she lives alone, she did not see that washing her clothing by hand was too much for her. She rationalized that that is how they did it in the old days. Troubled, you purchase and have a new washing machine delivered to Aunt Mary.

Some time has passed and you forgot to inquire of Aunt Mary if she liked having the new washing machine. You go to visit her only to find the tags still on the washing machine and Aunt Mary washing her clothing in the tub with her wash board. You ask her why she is still washing her clothing in the tub with a wash board and not using the new washing machine. You inform her that you purchased the washing machine to relieve her from washing her clothing manually. Aunt Mary replied that she was just used to doing it the old way.

What about you? Are you trying to accomplish the things of this life all on your own, when you have Christ who will and wants to do in you, through you, and for you what you find difficult and cannot do yourself?

"Do you not know that in a race all the runners run, but only one gets the prize? Run in such a way as to get the prize" (1 Corinthians 9:24). May God richly bless you as you run the race that has been marked out for you (Hebrews 12:2).

CHAPTER 14

A Personal Invitation

$\mathcal{Y}$ou will receive a variety of invitations during your lifetime and many that will spark pleasant anticipation. There is an invitation I would like to extend to you. Prayerfully, you have read through *The Christian Woman's Guide to a Blessed Life* and have found information that has been helpful to you. You may have noticed and even questioned the magnitude of Scripture. The Bible is God's Word. In it are His instructions for how we are to live. It is a book of life experiences. In the Bible are the answers to all of life's problems. The Scriptures and principles enclosed are what God used to teach and transform my family and me. While God is still conforming me to be like His Son and my Savior, Jesus, I would be remiss if I did not extend this invitation to YOU. Like Mary Magdalene and the other women who faithfully loved following Jesus, won't you join me and follow Jesus too? I cannot promise you that there will not be difficult moments.

Many years ago, I was attending a women's conference with a friend in California. While we were in our room together, I asked her how to obtain a deeper walk with Christ and she responded, "Sharie, you just have to jump." That was a scary truth for me at that moment. I wanted to, but who would catch me and could I trust Jesus to keep me? I can recall mentally tossing the idea back and forth, but I cannot remember the actual moment I thrust myself from the cliff of camouflaged safety into the hands of Jesus. Since that time, God has brought about and allowed the circumstances of my life to illuminate my need for Him and deepen my faith.

I am a fearful person by nature. My journey of trust was a slow process in the beginning due to my fear. I do not know who you are or what your struggles may be, but what I do know is that no matter where you are in life, you can trust Jesus. I did and I found Him to be a faithful friend. To trust Jesus is a decision only you can make. No one can do it for you. But neither can you experience God's wonderful and supernatural plan for your life if you don't take the plunge of faith. Let me encourage you. It is Satan who does not want you take this step of faith to trust Jesus for your life. He knows that the moment you do, he will no longer have any power over you.

Before my second son was born, I was told I would have to have a spinal tap (all of my children were born by Cesarean section). I had two weeks before his scheduled delivery, but I had to make my decision immediately for medical preparation purposes. Fearful, my husband prayed with me that night. I awoke early the following morning with this song on my lips, "Be not dismayed whatever betide you. Beneath His wings of love abide, God will take care of you." Within one hour, I went into labor—two weeks before my scheduled delivery time.

My three-year old had to go with us due to the hour and nature of the situation. Fearfully, I thought who would be with me? My husband had to stay with our other son. Then that which I dreaded most came. In the surgical room, they proceeded to administer the spinal medication. Fearful and shaking, the doctors said I had to lie still. At that moment, afraid without my husband by my side, I had to make a decision whether I would trust God with my life. Turning to Jesus with tears rolling down my cheeks, I prayed, "Dear Jesus, please help me." I closed my eyes and visualized jumping into His arms. What was to follow changed my life. I was immediately filled with a peace that was beyond anything I had ever known, while my mind was filled with words and tunes from hymns I had learned as a child.

Not all of your experiences will be what Christians call, "mountaintop experiences." He just has a way in your most needed hour of letting you know He is near. There will be times you may even question His presence, but He promises to be with you, that He will never leave or forsake you.

You have heard my story, now what about you? I pray that God will give you the strength to step forward and take your stand with me and many others who have come to know the blessings of knowing Jesus as Savior and Lord.

After having heard the truth of the gospel, Jesus wants to give you the opportunity to respond by opening your heart and receiving Him as your personal Savior and Lord. He loves you and has a wonderful plan for your life. You can receive that love and come to know that plan by praying this simple prayer: Dear Jesus, I need You. Please forgive and cleanse me of all sin. Come into my heart and save me. I give You my heart and life. Make me the woman you want me to be. Thank You for coming into my life today and giving me a new beginning.

Now that you have become a Christian, here are some helpful tips that will help you on your journey:

1. You can be sure that God heard and answered your prayer by reading the following Scriptures: John 3:16; John 1:12; Romans 10:9–13; 1 John 5:13–15; Revelation 3:20.
2. Next, it is important that you unite with a church that preaches and teaches the Bible.
3. Read your Bible daily for developing your new life in Christ (2 Corinthians 5:17).
4. Remember God loves you and nothing can separate you from His love (Roman 8:38).
5. For more details (see HM-9), "The Key to a Victorious Christian Life."

May God bless you as you trust and journey through life with Jesus!

SAMPLES AND FORMS

HM-1
PRIORITY LIST SAMPLE

AS A CHRISTIAN

- Daily devotions (Bible reading and personal prayer)
- Church worship
- Tithing
- Sunday school
- Bible study
- Ministry involvement
- Witnessing
- Community affairs
- Prayer

AS A WOMAN (Personal)

- Diet (eating right)
- Exercise
- Hygiene (bathing, hair and teeth)
- Education for personal growth (reading or formal education)
- Talents, hobbies, interests
- Fellowship with other Christian women

AS A WIFE (Helpmate)

- The above (As a Woman)
- Loving mate (physically, emotionally, spiritually, socially, and financially)
- Home management (cleaning, washing, shopping, and cooking)
- Business (finances, major home purchases, and administration)
- Learning new ways to become a better wife

AS A MOTHER

- Teaching (introduce new principles for mental, physical, emotional, and spiritual growth)
- Training (walking alongside your child(ren) and allowing them to walk alongside of you to perfect lessons learned)
- Nurturing (words and acts of affirmation to strengthen your child(ren)'s self-image)
- Discipline (correction)
- Involved, supportive, and attentive to children's activities
- Joining the Parent and School Association
- Learning new ways to become a better mother
- Meeting with other moms

HM-2A
ADULT WEEKLY SCHEDULE SAMPLE

Sunday	Monday	Tuesday	Wednesday	Thursday	Friday	Saturday	Notes
Devotion	Devotion	Devotion	Devotion	Devotion	Devotion	Devotion	
Shower	Reading 1 Hour	Reading 1 Hour	Reading 1 Hour	Reading 1 Hour	Reading 1 Hour	Stay in bed with husband	
Get Dressed	Wash & Iron			Wash & Iron			
Make-up	Pack lunches	Pack lunches	Pack Lunches	Pack lunches	Pack lunches		
Dress kids	Breakfast with kids	Breakfast with kids	Breakfast with kids	Breakfast With kids	Breakfast with kids	Family breakfast	
Worship	Room & bath check	Room & bath check	Room & bath check	Room & bath check	Room & bath check	Kids events	
Sunday School	Devotion with kids	Devotion with kids	Devotion with kids	Devotion With kids	Devotion with kids	Meet w/friend 1x per month	
4TH Sunday meeting	Wash & iron	House cleaning	Class or Bible Study Lesson	Wash & Iron	Groceries (every other week)	Family dinner (on their own)	
Family Dinner	Noon prayer	Noon prayer	Noon Prayer	Noon prayer	Write family (every other week)	Relax	
Nap	Dinner prep	Dinner prep	Dinner Prep	Dinner Prep	Family House cleaning		
Evening worship	Snack with kids	Snack with kids	Snack with kids	Snack With kids	Family Night		
	Homework with kids	Homework with kids	Homework with kids	Homework With kids	Games		
	Dinner	Dinner	Dinner	Dinner	Special dinner		
Snack with Family	Read to kids	Class or Bible Lesson	Bible Study	Meet out With Husband	Family play time	Family devotion	
Kids to bed	Exercise Shower	Exercise Shower	Exercise Shower	Evening with husband	Fun!!!!!	Family worship prep.	
Prayer Bed	Prayer Bed	Prayer Bed	Prayer Bed	Prayer Bed	Prayer Bed	Prayer Bed	

HM-2b
ADULT WEEKLY SCHEDULE SAMPLE

SUNDAY

Devotion
Shower
Breakfast prep.
Get dressed
Sunday School
Church Worship
Dinner
Nap
Evening Worship
Family dessert
Kids to bed
Personal grooming
Prayer/bed

MONDAY

Devotion
Breakfast
Devotion w/kids
1 hr. reading
Wash/Iron
Dinner prep.
Bake weekly dessert
Mtg. W/kid #1
Homework w/kids
Kid training night
Kids to bed
Pack lunches
Exercise
Personal grooming
Bible reading
Prayer/bed

TUESDAY

Devotion
Get dresses
Make bed
Breakfast prep.
Devotion w/kids
Wash/Iron
Dinner prep.
Homework w/kids
Dinner
Mtg. W/kid #2
Kids to bed
Pack lunches
Exercise
Personal grooming
Bible reading
Prayer/bed

WEDNESDAY

Devotion
Make bed
Get dressed
Breakfast prep.
Devotion w/kids
1 hr. reading
Straighten house
Dinner prep.
Ministry prep.
Homework w/kids
Dinner
Bible Study
Snack for kids
Kids to bed
Personal grooming
Evening w/ husband

THURSDAY

Devotion
Make bed
Get dressed
Breakfast prep.
Devotion w/kids
Straighten house
Dinner prep.
Homework w/kids
Dinner
Games w/kids
Kids to bed
Pack lunches
Exercise
Personal grooming
Prayer/bed

FRIDAY

Devotion
Make bed
Get dressed
Breakfast prep.
Devotion w/kids
1 hr. reading
Clean kitchen
Banking(twice per month)
Groceries(twice per month)
Kids to library
House cleaning
Family Night

SATURDAY

Devotion
Family Breakfast
Kids activities (sport, music etc.)
FREE AFTERNOON
Fellowship w/ friend (1) per month
Personal outing or shopping
Write letters or send cards
Time w/ extended family
Family devotion
Worship prep.
Prayer/bed

HM-2c
CHILD'S WEEKLY SCHEDULE SAMPLE

Sunday	Monday	Tuesday	Wednesday
__ Wake up	__ Wake up	__ Wake up	__ Wake up
__ Prayer	__ Prayer	__ Prayer	__ Prayer
__ Make bed	__ Make bed	__ Make bed	__ Make bed
__ Wash face	__ Shower	__ Shower	__ Shower
__ Brush teeth	__ Brush teeth	__ Brush teeth	__ Brush teeth
__ Get dressed	__ Deodorant	__ Deodorant	__ Deodorant
__ Breakfast	__ Lotion body	__ Lotion body	__ Lotion body
	__ Get dressed	__ Get dressed	__ Get dressed
. clear table	__ Straighten room	__ Straighten room	__ Straighten room
	__ Brush hair	__ Brush hair	__ Brush hair
__ Brush hair	__ School bag prep.	__ School bag prep.	__ School bag prep.
__ Straighten room			
__ Gather belongings	. 2 pencils	. 2 pencils	. 2 pencils
	. paper	. paper	. paper
. coat	. notebook	. notebook	. notebook
. Bible	. homework	. homework	. homework
. notebook	book	book	book
. offering	. trombone	. lunch	. art supplies
. name badge	. music folder		. lunch
	. lunch	__ Breakfast	
__ Sunday School			__ Breakfast
__ Church worship	__ Breakfast	. clear dishes	
__ Dinner			. clear dishes
__ Nap	. clear dishes	__ Devotion	
__ Class		__ Bathroom	__ Devotion
__ Evening worship	__ Devotion	__ Put on coat	__ Bathroom
__ Dressed for bed	__ Bathroom	__ School (8:30)	__ Coat
__ Snack	__ Coat	__ Hang up coat	__ School
__ Prayer	__ School(8:30)	__ Put away lunch	__ Hang up coat
__ Bed	__ Hang up coat	__ Pull all papers	__ Put away lunch
	__ Put away lunch	__ Snack	__ Pull all papers
	__ Pull all papers	__ Homework	__ Snack
	__ Snack	__ Music lessons	__ Homework
	__ Homework	__ Dinner	__ Music lessons
	__ Dinner	__ Wash dishes	__ Dinner
	__ Wash dishes	__ Meeting w/ mom	__ Wash dishes
	__ Training	__ Wash face	__ Bathroom
	__ Wash face	brush teeth	__ Bible/coat
	brush teeth	__ P.J.'s	__ Bible Study
	__ P.J.'s	__ Take clothes out	__ Wash face
	__ Take clothes out	for school	brush teeth
	for school	__ Straighten room	__ P.J.'s
	__ Straighten room	__ Prayer	__ Take clothes
	__ Prayer	__ Bed	__ Prayer
	__ Bed	__ Bible reading	__ Bed
	__ Bible reading		

HM–2c (CONTINUED)
CHILD'S WEEKLY SCHEDULE SAMPLE

THURSDAY	FRIDAY	SATURDAY
__ Wake up	__ Wake up	__ Wake up
__ Prayer	__ Prayer	__ Prayer
__ Make bed	__ Make bed	__ Strip bed
__ Shower	__ Shower	__ Shower
. brush teeth	. brush teeth	. brush teeth
. deodorant	. deodorant	. deodorant
. lotion body	. lotion body	. lotion body
__ Get dressed	__ Get dressed	__ Get dressed
__ Straighten room	__ Straighten room	__ Straighten room
__ Brush hair	__ Brush hair	__ Brush hair
__ School bag	__ School bag	__ Breakfast
		__ Music lessons
. 2 pencils	. 2 pencils	__ Play day
. paper	. paper	__ Dinner
. notebook	. notebook	__ Hair cut
. homework	. homework	__ Bath
book	book	__ Wash hair
. recorder	. art supplies	__ Worship prep.
. lunch	. lunch	
		. clothes out
__ Breakfast	__ Breakfast	. tithes &
		offerings
. clear dishes	. clear dishes	. Bible
__ Devotion	__ Devotion	__ Family devotion
__ Bathroom	__ Bathroom	__ Snack
__ Coat	__ Coat	__ Prayer
__ School (8:30)	__ School (8:30)	__ Bed
__ Hang up coat	__ Hang up coat	
__ Put away lunch	__ Put away lunch	
__ Pull all papers	__ Pull all papers	
__ Snack	__ Library	
__ Homework	__ Chores	
__ Music lessons	__ Family Night	
__ Dinner		
. clear table		
. wash dishes		
__ Wash face		
. brush teeth		
__ P.J.'s		
__ Clothes out		
for school		
__ Game		
__ Prayer		
__ Bed		
__ Bible reading		

HM-2D
ADULT WEEKLY SCHEDULE FORM

Sunday	Monday	Tuesday	Wednesday	Thursday	Friday	Saturday	Notes

HM-3A
MONTHLY CALENDAR SAMPLE

May

Sunday	Monday	Tuesday	Wednesday	Thursday	Friday	Saturday
			Bible Study	Mtg. w/ Husband (marriage)	School Trip Groceries	Music Choir Gymnastics
Worship Commu-nion	Pool cleaned Class	Mail Ministry Brochures	Bible Study Parent Ass. Mtg.	Hair appt.Mtg. w/Husband (children)	Write Bills Library	Music Choir Gymnastics
Worship Evening Worship	Class	Dad Doctors	Bible Study	Mtg. w/ Husband (finances)	Groceries	Husband Class Mtg w/friend
Worship Evening Worship	Derma Orthodontist Class		Airport Bible study	School Performance	Write bills Orthoped	Seminar
Worship Ministry mtg.	Class	Family Dentist	Clean carpet Bible study	Mtg. w/ Husband (fun)	Youth retreat	

HM–3b
MONTHLY CALENDAR FORM

Month of_____

Sunday	Monday	Tuesday	Wednesday	Thursday	Friday	Saturday

HM-4A
THINGS-TO-DO-LIST SAMPLE

DATE_____

PRIORITY	THINGS TO DO
1	WASH
_____	_____
	IRON
_____	_____
2	DEVOTION
_____	_____
3	DINNER PREP
_____	_____
5	DINNER
_____	_____
4	STORE (MILK AND JUICE)
_____	_____
4	CHILD TO ORTHODONTIST
_____	_____
6	MEETING WITH HUSBAND
_____	_____
7	READING
_____	_____

HM-4B
THINGS-TO-DO LIST FORM

DATE_____

PRIORITY   **THINGS TO DO**

_____   _____

_____   _____

_____   _____

_____   _____

_____   _____

_____   _____

_____   _____

_____   _____

HM-5A
MEAL AND GROCERY
PLANNING SCHEDULE SAMPLE

February

Sunday	Monday	Tuesday	Wednesday	Thursday	Friday	Saturday
Roast Potatoes Corn Salad	Beans & Rice, Italian sausage Corn muffins	Baked chicken Beans & Rice Muffins	Linguine w/Chicken breast & Mushrooms Salad Bread	Chicken Pot Pie	Pizza Chips Soda and Candy	Fish Fry-French fries Coleslaw
Lasagna Salad & rolls	Lasagna Green beans Rolls	Clam Chowder Hamburgers	Clam Chowder Salad Rolls	Salad Hot dogs Baked beans Spinach	Buffalo Wings Celery & Pot. Salad	Deli Sandwiches, Chips w/pickle

HM-5B
MEAL AND GROCERY
PLANNING SCHEDULE FORM

Month of _____

Sunday	Monday	Tuesday	Wednesday	Thursday	Friday	Saturday

HM-6
GROCERY LIST FORM

Date_____

QTY	PRODUCT	COST	CATEGORY	COUPON (X=Yes)
	MILK		DAIRY	
	AMERICAN CHEESE		DAIRY	
	MOZARELLA CHEESE		DAIRY	
	COTTAGE CHEESE		DAIRY	
	CREAM CHEESE		DAIRY	
	BUTTER MILK		DAIRY	
	SOUR CREAM		DAIRY	
	EGGS		DAIRY	
	ICE CREAM		DAIRY	
	BUTTER		DAIRY	
	YOGURT		DAIRY	
	LUNCHMEAT		MEAT	
	BACON		MEAT	
	SAUSAGE-LINK		MEAT	
	SAUSAGE-PATTY		MEAT	
	CHICKEN		MEAT	
	ROAST		MEAT	
	GROUND BEEF		MEAT	
	TURKEY		MEAT	
	TUNA		MEAT	
	HAM		MEAT	
	HOT DOGS		MEAT	
	RIBS		MEAT	
	STEAK		MEAT	
	PORK CHOPS		MEAT	
	LIVER		MEAT	
	LETTUCE		PRODUCE	
	TOMATO		PRODUCE	
	ONION		PRODUCE	

GROCERY LIST FORM

Date_____

QTY	PRODUCT	COST	CATEGORY	COUPON (X=Yes)
	CUCUMBER		PRODUCE	
	PEPPERS(GR, RED,YEL)		PRODUCE	
	RADISH		PRODUCE	
	SCALLIONS		PRODUCE	
	MUSHROOMS		PRODUCE	
	DRESSING-RUSSIAN		CONDIMENTS	
	DRESSING-BL. CHEESE		CONDIMENTS	
	DRESSING-FRENCH		CONDIMENTS	
	DRESSING-ITALIAN		CONDIMENTS	
	DRESSING-1000 ISL.		CONDIMENTS	
	APPLES		FRUIT	
	BANANAS		FRUIT	
	PEARS		FRUIT	
	GRAPES		FRUIT	
	PEACHES		FRUIT	
	WATERMELON		FRUIT	
	NECTARINES		FRUIT	
	PLUMS		FRUIT	
	ORANGES		FRUIT	
	JUICE-ORANGE		BEVERAGE	
	JUICE-APPLE		BEVERAGE	
	JUICE-CRAN/APPLE		BEVERAGE	
	JUICE-GRAPEFRUIT		BEVERAGE	
	JUICE-PRUNE		BEVERAGE	
	GREEN BEANS		VEGETABLE	
	BROCCOLI		VEGETABLE	
	BEANS		VEGETABLE	
	CABBAGE		VEGETABLE	
	BEETS		VEGETABLE	

GROCERY LIST FORM

Date_____

QTY	PRODUCT	COST	CATEGORY	COUPON (X=Yes)
	CORN		VEGETABLE	
	POTATOES (SW,WH)		VEGETABLE	
	SQUASH		VEGETABLE	
	TURNIPS		VEGETABLE	
	GREENS (TURN/COLL)		VEGETABLE	
	SPINACH		VEGETABLE	
	PEAS		VEGETABLE	
	ASPARAGUS		VEGETABLE	
	TOMATO SAUCE		CANNED GOODS	
	TOMATO PASTE		CANNED GOODS	
	CRUSHED TOMATO		CANNED GOODS	
	KETCHUP		CONDIMENT	
	MUSTARD		CONDIMENT	
	RELISH		CONDIMENT	
	PORK&BEANS		CANNED GOODS	
	APPLESAUCE		CANNED GOODS	
	SOUP		CANNED GOODS	
	CHOCOLATE		BAKING	
	OIL		BAKING	
	SOY SAUCE		CONDIMENT	
	WORCESTER SAUCE		CONDIMENT	
	SYRUP		CONDIMENT	
	HOT SAUCE		CONDIMENT	
	JAM/JELLY		CONDIMENT	
	PEANUTBUTTER		CONDIMENT	
	KIDNEY BEANS		CANNED GOODS	
	PAPER TOWELS		PAPER GOODS	
	TOILET TISSUE		PAPER GOODS	
	NAPKINS		PAPER GOODS	

GROCERY LIST FORM

Date_____

QTY	PRODUCT	COST	CATEGORY	COUPON (X=Yes)
	GARBAGE BAG-SM/LG		PAPER GOODS	
	SANDWICH BAGS		PAPER GOODS	
	FREEZER BAGS		PAPER GOODS	
	LUNCH BAGS		PAPER GOODS	
	ALUMINUM FOIL		PAPER GOODS	
	PLASTIC WRAP		PAPER GOODS	
	BAR SOAP		TOILETRIES	
	DISHWASHING LIQ.		CLEANING	
	DISHWASHER DETER.		CLEANING	
	DETERGENT		CLEANING	
	FABRIC SOFTENER		CLEANING	
	SPRAY STARCH		CLEANING	
	BLEACH		CLEANING	
	SPIC-N-SPAN		CLEANING	
	MOP-N-GLO		CLEANING	
	FURNITURE POLISH		CLEANING	
	GLASS CLEANER		CLEANING	
	AIR FRESHNER		CLEANING	
	CREAM OF WHEAT		GRAIN	
	OATMEAL		GRAIN	
	GRITS		GRAIN	
	BOX CEREAL		GRAIN	
	CORN MEAL		BAKING	
	BREAD CRUMBS		BAKING	
	CRACKERS-RITZ		SNACK FOOD	
	CRACKERS-SALTINE		SNACK FOOD	
	CRACKERS-GRAHAM		SNACK FOOD	
	BREAD		BREAD	
	BUNS-HOT DOG		BREAD	

GROCERY LIST FORM

Date_____

QTY	PRODUCT	COST	CATEGORY	COUPON (X=Yes)
	BUNS-HAMBURGER		BREAD	
	BAGELS		BREAD	
	MUFFINS-ENGLISH		BREAD	
	PANCAKE MIX		BAKING	
	FLOUR		BAKING	
	YEAST		BAKING	
	RICE		STARCH	
	EGG NOODLES		STARCH	
	LASAGNA		STARCH	
	SPAGHETTI		STARCH	
	MACARONI		STARCH	
	LINGUINI		STARCH	
	VANILLA		SPICE	
	ANISE		SPICE	
	BAY LEAVES		SPICE	
	BASIL		SPICE	
	PARSLEY		SPICE	
	OREGANO		SPICE	
	OINION POWDER		SPICE	
	GARLIC POWDER		SPICE	
	CINNAMON		SPICE	
	GINGER		SPICE	
	PUMPKIN SPICE		SPICE	
	SALT		SPICE	
	PEPPER		SPICE	
	NUTMEG		SPICE	
	CORN STARCH		BAKING	
	SUGAR-WHITE		BAKING	
	SUGAR-BROWN		BAKING	

GROCERY LIST FORM

Date_____

QTY	PRODUCT	COST	CATEGORY	COUPON (X=Yes)
	SUGAR-POWDERED		BAKING	
	PAPRIKA		SPICE	
	CELERY SALT		SPICE	
	TOOTH PASTE		TOILETRIES	
	MOUTHWASH		TOILETRIES	
	DENTAL FLOSS		TOILETRIES	
	DEODORANT		TOILETRIES	
	RAZORS		TOILETRIES	
	ALCOHOL		TOILETRIES	
	Q-TIPS		TOILETRIES	
	COTTON BALLS		TOILETRIES	
	PAPER CUPS		PAPER	
	VASELINE		TOILETRIES	
	LOTION		TOILETRIES	
	BABY OIL		TOILETRIES	
	SHAMPOO		TOILETRIES	
	CONDITIONER		TOILETRIES	
	HAIR OIL		TOILETRIES	
	CHOCOLATE CHIPS		BAKING	
	CAKE MIX		BAKING	
	ICING		BAKING	
	COCONUT		BAKING	
	COCOA		BAKING	
	NUTS		BAKING	
	TEA		BEVERAGE	
	COFFEE		BEVERAGE	
	LIGHT BULBS		MISCELLANEOUS	
	MOP		MISCELLANEOUS	
	BROOM		MISCELLANEOUS	

GROCERY LIST FORM

Date_____

QTY	PRODUCT	COST	CATEGORY	COUPON (X=Yes)
	CANDY		SNACKS	
	FRUIT SNACKS		SNACKS	
	POPCORN		SNACKS	
	Total Cost			

HM-7

Financial Plan

For the Year_____

Month_____

Scripture: I Timothy 6:17

Description	Monthly	Bi-Monthly			
		Actual	15th Budget	Actual	30th Budget
Tithes					
Offering					
Savings					
Mortgage					
Groceries					
Telephone					
Utility-Electric					
Utility-Gas					
Water					
Car Payment					
Car Insurance					
Gas for Car					
Hairdresser					
Hair-Cut					
Dry Cleaners					
Stamps/Magazines					
Allowance					
Cable					
Mobile Phone					
Sub-total					
Credit					
Credit					
Credit					
Other					
Sub-total					
Total					
Income					
Income					
Total					
Income minus Expenses					

HM-8
WEEKLY/MONTHLY/QUARTERLY
COST SHEET FORM

	Budget	Actual
Week #1	_____	_____
Week #2	_____	_____
Week #3	_____	_____
Week #4	_____	_____

Total Month _____   _____

Week #1	_____	_____
Week #2	_____	_____
Week #3	_____	_____
Week #4	_____	_____

Total Month _____   _____

Week #1	_____	_____
Week #2	_____	_____
Week #3	_____	_____
Week #4	_____	_____

Total Month _____   _____

TOTAL QUARTER _____   _____

HM-9
THE KEY TO A VICTORIOUS CHRISTIAN LIFE

Read the Word of God—Daily
   Acts 17:11
   Psalm 1:1–2
   Psalm 119:11

Pray—Daily
   Psalm 86:3
   Psalm 88:9
   1 Thessalonians 5:17

Depend Upon God—Daily
   Psalm 25:5; 130:5
   Lamentation 3:24–25
   Luke 11:2–3

Die to Self—Daily
   1 Corinthians 15:31
   2 Corinthians 4:10

Take Up Your Cross—Daily
   Luke 9:23
   John 8:12

Confess Your Sins—Daily
   Psalm 31:5
   Proverbs 28:13
   1 John 1:9

Praise the Lord—Daily
   Job 1:21
   Psalm 119:164

1.   Jordan, *The Key to a Victorious Christian Life*

Sources

Prefaces

1. Department of Health and Human Services. Office on Women's Health: The Health of Minority Women. July 2003. *http://www.4women. gov/owh/pub/minority/index.htm.* February 5, 2004
2. Harris, Louis and Associates Inc. 1998 Survey of Women's Health. The Commonwealth Fund: May 1999. *http://www.cmwf.org/programs/women/ksc_whsurvey99_332.asp.*
3. Winfrey, Oprah. *Suburban Moms Addicted to Drugs.* Chicago: November 19, 2003.

Introduction

1. Goeringer, Conrad F. Madalyn Murray O'Hair Family Generations in Service to Atheism and the Separation of Church and State. July22,2003 *http://www.atheists.org/visitors.center/OHair-Family*.
2. Foster, Julie. *The Real 'Jane Roe' Famed Abortion Lawsuit Plaintiff Says Uncaring Attorneys 'Used' Her.* WorldNetDaily.com. February 4, 2001. Retrieved November 3, 2002 from World-NetDaily.com on the World Wide Web: *http://www.abortiontv.com/JaneRoe*.
3. Lanker, Brian. *I Dream A World*. New York: Stewart, Tabori & Chang, 1999, p. 78.
4. Janney, Rebecca Price. Great Women in American History. Camphill: Horizon Books, 1996, p. 197.

Chapter Two

1. Evangelical Training Association, *Biblical Beliefs*. Wheaton: ETA, 1982, pp. 14–16.

Chapter Four

1. Brazelton, T. Berry, M.D. and Sparrow, Joshua D., M.D. *Sleeping, The Brazelton Way*. Cambridge: Perseus Publishing, 2003, pp. 63–67.

2. Zodhiates, Spiros Th.D. *The Hebrew Greek Key Word Study Bible*. Chattanooga: AMG, 1996, pp. 1931,1981.

Chapter Eight

1. Freeman, James M. *Manners and Customs of the Bible*. Plainfield: Logos International, 1972, pp. 162–163.

Chapter Twelve

1. Sinnigen, William G. "Cleopatra." *World Book Encyclopedia*. Chicago: World Book, Inc. 1991, ed., p. 662.
2. Lockyer, Dr. Herbert, *All the Women of the Bible*. Grand Rapids: Zondervan, 1991, p. 14.
3. Goeringer, Conrad F. *Madalyn Murray O'Hair Family Generations in Service to Atheism and the Separation of Church and State*. July 22,2003. *http://www.atheists.org/visitors.center/OHairFamily*
4. Carson, Ben M.D. and Murphey, Cecil. *Gifted Hands*. Grand Rapids: Zondervan, 1992.

HM-9

1. Jordan, Robert E. *The Key to a Victorious Christian Life*. Lansdale: Calvary Baptist Church.

Recommended Reading

PERSONAL LIFE

A Heart for God by D. Stuart Briscoe - (Zondervan)

Embraced by the Cross Discovering the Principles of Christian Faith and Life by L.E. Maxwell - (Moody Press)

Hinds Feet in High Places by Hannah Hurnard - (Tyndale House)

How to Listen to God by Charles Stanley - (Thomas Nelson)

Hudson Taylor by J. Hudson Taylor - (Bethany House)

Ordering Your Private World by Gordan MacDonald - (Thomas Nelson)

The Calvary Road by Roy Hession - (Christian Literature Crusade)

The Wonderful Spirit Filled Life by Charles Stanley - (Thomas Nelson)

AS A WOMAN

Discover Your Spiritual Gift and Use It by Rick Yohn - (Tyndale House)

Emotional Phases of a Woman's Life by Jean Lush with Patricia H. Rushford - (Fleming H. Revell Co.)

Personality Plus by Florence Littauer - (Fleming H. Revell Co.)

HOME MANAGEMENT

Balancing Life's Demands by J. Grant Howard - (Multnomah Press)

The Messies Superguide by Sandra Felton - (Fleming H. Revell Co.)

Tyranny of the Urgent by Charles E. Hummel - (Intervarsity Christian Fellowship)

It Only Hurts Between Paydays by Amy Ross Mumford - (Accent Books)

AS A WIFE

The Act of Marriage by Tim and Beverly LaHaye - (Zondervan)

God's Armor Bearer by Terry Nance - (Harrison House)

How to Practice Real Love by Dr. Willie Richardson - (Christian Research & Development)

Me? Obey Him? by Elizabeth Rice Handford - (Sword of the Lord)

Understanding the Man in Your Life by H. Norman Wright - (Word Publishers)

AS A MOTHER

Growing Up God's Way by John A. Stormer - (Liberty Bell Press)

How to Develop Your Child's Temperament by Beverly La Haye - (Harvest House)

How to Really Love Your Child by Dr. Ross Campbell - (Victor Books)

How to Really Love Your Teenager by Dr. Ross Campbell - (Victor Books)

Preparing For Adolescence by Dr. James Dobson - (Regal Books)

Self-Counseling Workbook for Single Parents by Sheila Staley - (Christian Research & Development)

Taking Trauma Out of Teen Transition by Larry Anderson - (Nav Press)

Under Loving Command by Al and Pat Fabrizio - (Sheva Press)

COPING WITH STRESS

Boundaries Face to Face by Dr. Henry Cloud and Dr. John Townsend - (Zondervan)

How to Get Along with Difficult People by Florence Littauer - (Harvest House)

How to Win Over Depression by Tim LaHaye - (Zondervan)

How to Win Over Worry by John Haggai - (Harvest House)

The *Christian Woman's Guide to Blessed Life* is an extension of Influence, Inc. If this material has proven to be a blessing to you we would love to hear from you. You can do so by contacting us at:

Influence
P.O. Box 203
Wyncote, PA 19095
(215) 572-5897
Influenceinc.org